D1329918

Baldwin's talent as a teacher of writing shines through in *Writing Your Psychology Research Paper*. This crisp, practical book should be the first stop for students new to writing about the science of psychology.

—**Paul J. Silvia, PhD**, University of North Carolina at Greensboro

From research-based class papers to manuscripts for professional journals—this easy-to-read book provides a clear guide for any student (undergraduate or graduate) who wants to improve the quality of his or her writing and save time in the writing process.

—**Joshua K. Swift, PhD**, Idaho State University, Pocatello

Writing Your Psychology Research Paper

Concise Guides to Conducting Behavioral, Health, and Social Science Research Series

Designing and Proposing Your Research Project
    Jennifer Brown Urban and Bradley Matheus Van Eeden-Moorefield

Writing Your Psychology Research Paper
    Scott A. Baldwin

Writing Your Psychology Research Paper

SCOTT A. BALDWIN

CONCISE GUIDES TO CONDUCTING BEHAVIORAL,
HEALTH, AND SOCIAL SCIENCE RESEARCH

AMERICAN PSYCHOLOGICAL ASSOCIATION • *Washington, DC*

Published by
American Psychological Association
750 First Street, NE
Washington, DC 20002
www.apa.org

To order
APA Order Department
P.O. Box 92984
Washington, DC 20090-2984
Tel: (800) 374-2721; Direct: (202) 336-5510
Fax: (202) 336-5502; TDD/TTY: (202) 336-6123
Online: www.apa.org/pubs/books
E-mail: order@apa.org

In the U.K., Europe, Africa, and the Middle East, copies may be ordered from
American Psychological Association
3 Henrietta Street
Covent Garden, London
WC2E 8LU England

Typeset in Minion by Circle Graphics, Inc., Columbia, MD

Printer: Sheridan Books, Ann Arbor, MI
Cover Designer: Naylor Design, Washington, DC

The opinions and statements published are the responsibility of the authors, and such opinions and statements do not necessarily represent the policies of the American Psychological Association.

Library of Congress Cataloging-in-Publication Data

Names: Baldwin, Scott A., author.
Title: Writing your psychology research paper / Scott A. Baldwin.
Description: First edition. | Washington, DC : American Psychological
    Association, [2018] | Series: Concise guides to conducting behavioral,
    health, and social science research | Includes bibliographical references
    and index.
Identifiers: LCCN 2017003497 | ISBN 9781433827075 | ISBN 1433827077
Subjects: LCSH: Psychology—Authorship. | Psychology—Research. | Academic
    writing.
Classification: LCC BF76.7 .B35 2018 | DDC 808.06/615—dc23 LC record available at
    https://lccn.loc.gov/2017003497

British Library Cataloguing-in-Publication Data
A CIP record is available from the British Library.

Printed in the United States of America
First Edition

http://dx.doi.org/10.1037/0000045-000

To Will Shadish. I'll miss you.

Contents

CONTENTS

Series Foreword

Why are you reading this book? Perhaps you have recently been assigned to write a research paper in an undergraduate course. Maybe you are considering graduate school in one of the behavioral, health, or social science disciplines, such as psychology, public health, nursing, or medicine, and know that having a strong research background gives you a major advantage in getting accepted. Maybe you simply want to know how to conduct research in these areas. Or perhaps you are interested in actually conducting your own study. Regardless of the reason, you are probably wondering—how do I start?

Conducting research can be analogous to cooking a meal for several people. Doing so involves planning (e.g., developing a menu), having adequate resources (e.g., having the correct pots, pans, carving knives, plates), knowing what the correct ingredients are (e.g., what spices are needed), properly cooking the meal (e.g., grilling vs. baking, knowing how long it takes to cook), adequately presenting the food (e.g., making the meal look appetizing), and so forth. Conducting research also involves planning, proper execution, having adequate resources, and presenting one's project in a meaningful manner. Both activities also involve creativity, persistence, caring, and ethical behavior. But just like cooking a meal for several people, conducting research should follow one of my favorite pieces of advice—"remember that the devil is in the details." If you want your dinner guests to find your meal tasty, you need to follow a recipe properly and measure the ingredients accurately (e.g., too much or little of some of the ingredients can make the entrée taste awful). Similarly, conducting research without properly paying attention to details can lead to erroneous results.

Okay, but what about your question—"how do I start?" This American Psychological Association (APA) book series provides detailed but user-friendly guides for conducting research in the behavioral, health, and social sciences from start to finish. I cannot help but think of another food analogy here—that is, the series will focus on everything from "soup to nuts." These short, practical books will guide the student/researcher through each stage of the process of developing, conducting, writing, and presenting a research project. Each book will focus on a single aspect of research, for example, choosing a research topic, following ethical guidelines when conducting research with humans, using appropriate statistical tools to analyze your data, and deciding which measures to use in your project. Each volume in this series will help you attend to the details of a specific activity. All volumes will help you complete important tasks and will include illustrative examples. Although the theory and conceptualization behind each activity is important to know, these books will especially focus on the "how to" of conducting research, so that you, the research student, can successfully carry out a meaningful research project.

This particular volume, by Scott Baldwin, focuses on writing a research paper. All of the earlier parts of the process—the careful planning, assembling of "ingredients," preparing, and conducting the research—have led to this key part of scientific inquiry, presenting the findings to consumers of research. Thus, if you are ready to write your paper and need user-friendly guidelines, whether your paper involves a critical summary of a particular topic (e.g., effective treatments for anxiety) or a description of an actual research study you conducted, this book can be of immense aid.

So, the answer to the question "How do I start?" is simple: *Just turn the page and begin reading!*

Best of luck!

Arthur M. Nezu
Series Editor

Acknowledgments

I'd like to thank Will Shadish for asking me to write this book. Will was my major professor and mentor during graduate school. It is hard to overstate the impact he had on my career as well as my development as a writer. I still have a long way to go professionally, but Will's support, feedback, constructive criticism, and enthusiasm prepared me for an academic career far better than I could have imagined when I started my PhD. He was gracious enough to lend me some of the material he used for writing assignments in his undergraduate classes. This material greatly influenced the content of Chapters 3, 4, and 5. For example, I based the structure of the research summaries on his assignments, my descriptions of the parts of a research paper are based on his, and some of the rules I list for improving writing were taken from him.

Unfortunately, Will passed away while I was finishing the first draft. I'm disappointed that he never got to see this final book, mostly because I think he would have seen his influence in the way I think about writing. I'm grateful that Will mentored me during graduate school and the early part of my career. I'll miss his influence and wise words.

I'd also like to thank my wife, Autumn. She helped me become not only a better writer but also a better person. She's a constant in my life, and I can't imagine going through my ups and downs without her. I'm lucky to have met her, and I love her more than I know how to express.

My kids are the best: Jack, Thomas, Carter, James, and Lily. Often work is a grind, with meetings, writing, teaching, more meetings, and then usually more writing. I love my job, and I'm grateful for it. However, when it is a grind, I remind myself that I get to come home to listen to Jack play the guitar, go on a run with Carter and Thomas, watch James's basketball games, and read with Lily. That's awesome.

Writing Your Psychology Research Paper

Introduction

If you're reading this book, chances are you've been assigned a research paper in your psychology class, or maybe you're starting a senior thesis. My students have a wide range of responses to writing assignments, including excitement, dread, fear, curiosity, apathy, confidence, and the strong desire to drop the class. On the one hand, a research paper can let you dive deep into a topic you're interested in, which enhances your learning experience and enjoyment of a class. On the other hand, writing is hard work and sometimes even boring and tedious. The purpose of this book is to help you write your research paper—and to help you write it well. Specifically, this book will give you structure, advice, guidelines, and even some practice to help you write well, or at least better than before. In addition, I hope this book will help you tip the scales toward the writing assignment being a positive learning experience rather than drudgery.

http://dx.doi.org/10.1037/0000045-001
Writing Your Psychology Research Paper, by S. A. Baldwin
Copyright © 2018 by the American Psychological Association. All rights reserved.

My students tell me that writing research papers is hard for at least two reasons. First, a blank document is overwhelming—a 10-page paper feels unreachable, especially when the first page is coming along so slowly. Second, writing well—clear, coherent, and thoughtful prose—does not come naturally. Thus, they worry about both what they'll say that will fill 10 pages and how they'll say it. They worry about the grammar rules they've learned since grade school and whether they'll remember when to say *less* and when to say *fewer*. I understand, and I'm sympathetic, but I'm reluctant to stop assigning papers. Learning to write clearly is fundamental to a college education, and few come to college (or graduate school or even their jobs) as good writers. Writers get better by writing, by receiving feedback, and by writing more.

My wife and I dated during college. Autumn was 2 years ahead of me, an English major, and a great writer. I was worried about a one-page essay for a philosophy class because I had received a bad grade on my first essay. She offered to critique my draft and help me revise it. I handed her the paper and watched TV while she worked. She eviscerated it—no sentence was left untouched, and everything needed to be reworked. She helped straighten out my use of the passive voice, helped make the tone professional, and cleaned up my use of tenses. The revised paper was better, and so was the grade I received.

After that semester, I wanted to get better at writing, so I enrolled in an advanced writing class with the best writer I could find—Daniel Graham, in my college's philosophy department. This was the hardest class I took as an undergraduate. Each essay, though short, required hours and hours of work. I wrote and rewrote. Dr. Graham was exacting and tough, and often my papers required extra revision beyond my initial drafts. That is how I got better. I learned how to craft an argument, how to get to the point, and how not to repeat myself. I learned to take the feedback as feedback, not as personal criticism.

My writing development didn't end with Dr. Graham's philosophy class. When I submitted the first draft of my master's thesis to my advisor, Will Shadish, I thought I had a solid draft and expected some feedback and edits, but nothing major. It turned out that nearly every paragraph needed work. I had sections that weren't connected to anything else. I was redundant. I didn't do a good job explaining ideas. After the initial shock of all the changes I had in front of me, I sat down to make it better, and it got better. I got better. I still do a lot of rewriting. I still have redundancies and gaps in my logic. But I got better with practice, and you will too.

Part of becoming a better writer is appreciating the process of writing and recognizing that the process of drafting, organizing, rewriting, and editing is what produces better writing and better writers. My hobby is triathlon, which consists of races that include swimming, biking, and running. Some races are short: swim 0.5 mile, bike 13 miles, and run 3.1 miles. Some races are long: swim 1.2 miles, bike 56 miles, and run 13.1 miles. And some races are insane: swim 2.4 miles, bike 112 miles, and run 26.2 miles. You could show up to a short triathlon without doing much training and finish the race. It might not be pretty, but you could probably get through most of it. The longer races, however, require training, and lots of it. Just getting through a 2.4-mile swim in a lake or ocean requires a level of fitness and comfort in the open water that only training can provide. After you finish the swim, you still need enough energy to bike 112 miles and then run a marathon. If you want to finish a long triathlon, you have to train. If you want to get better at triathlon, regardless of the distance, you have to embrace training and even enjoy it. Training is how you improve, and races are where you get to see how much you've improved.

Writing is similar, except without the muscle cramps, spandex, and profuse sweating. When you get a small writing assignment, such as a reaction paper or a short-answer exam question, you can probably just show up and get through the assignment. It may not be the best writing you could produce, but it will likely get the job done. However, when you get a longer writing assignment, just showing up and hoping you'll get through it usually leads to a crappy paper. Longer papers require drafting, organizing, rewriting, and editing—these steps are training for writers. Getting better at writing of any length requires training. When I was a student, a 10-page paper made me anxious and was a complete slog. Now hardly a week goes by in which I don't write 10 pages. That transition didn't happen overnight; it's OK for writing to be hard and to take time. I finished second-to-last in my age group in my first triathlon. Since that time, I've embraced training, and last fall I was first in my age group at a local race.

Remember that practicing writing isn't only about getting through one paper. The practice is to make your paper better but also to make all of your writing better. I no longer just train for a single triathlon. To be sure, I work toward specific races and want to do well at them, but I train to be a better swimmer, cyclist, and runner. That's what makes training fun and challenging. Practice writing to become a better writer. You'll write better class papers, exam answers, and blog posts. If you go to graduate school, you'll be better prepared to write your thesis and dissertation. If you enter the workforce, you'll be better prepared to write progress reports and business plans. Most people aren't good writers—you'll stand out.

Even if you're more concerned with getting through the paper at hand than with improving your writing in general, you'll benefit from the ideas and direction in this book. To guide the discussion, I will assume that you've been assigned to write a typical psychology research paper. In this kind of paper, you focus on a single idea—for example, the biological basis of obsessive–compulsive disorder—and you review, evaluate, and synthesize the research on the topic. The examples in this book assume that your assignment requires you to review articles and books on your topic, but the examples can be generalized to papers for which you've collected data and must synthesize the new data with existing data. Furthermore, many of the topics can be generalized to other types of writing assignments, such as reaction papers. To help you adapt the material to other assignments, I have included exhibits that describe ways you can adjust the material in this book to different kinds of assignments.

This book is divided into three parts. Part I covers preparing to write. Chapter 1 covers how to develop an idea for your paper, and Chapter 2 covers how to search for background information and literature. Part II covers writing. Chapter 3 covers prewriting, including organizing your background information, developing a thesis or primary aim for your paper, and using outlines and mind maps. Chapter 4 covers how to structure a paper and how to start drafting. Chapter 5 covers revising your paper and provides tips for improving your writing. Chapter 6 covers creating a bibliography and avoiding plagiarism. I also review software options that ease the process of creating a bibliography. Part III includes a single chapter on procrastination. Procrastination, more than any other behavior, stifles good writing. We need to talk about it.

This book is, by design, brief. I don't pretend to be exhaustive, nor do I cover all possible methods for writing a research paper. The methods I discuss in this book have worked for me and my students. If I try to write while skipping these methods—for example, if I try to write without a clear thesis in mind—then my writing suffers. I have observed the same problem with my students. Clear writing produces clear thinking, and clear writing comes from hard work. Let's get working.

ONE

PREPARING TO WRITE

1

Developing an Idea

Without a doubt, the most common question I hear from students about research papers is, "What should I write about?" It's not a trivial concern. If you don't have a good idea, you likely won't end up with a good paper, both in terms of getting a good grade and, more importantly, in terms of having a good learning experience. Writing is hard enough even when you care about the topic; it's a chore when you're stuck with a boring idea. (Granted, what is boring to one person is the life's work of another—after all, I'm one of the few people on Earth who find statistics fascinating—but you want a topic that isn't boring to you.) This chapter will help you use brainstorming to generate ideas and then give you tips for how to develop one of those ideas into a specific research topic.

A word of caution: Beware the appeal of the first idea that comes to mind. Yes, you need to develop an idea and actually write the paper, and the first idea is often appealing because it solves the problem of what to

http://dx.doi.org/10.1037/0000045-002
Writing Your Psychology Research Paper, by S. A. Baldwin

write about. Remember, however, that having an idea doesn't mean that it's a good idea or that you'll be sufficiently motivated by it to see the paper through. Relief that you've come up with something to write about doesn't equal excitement or enthusiasm. Write the idea down, continue brainstorming, and if the first idea still seems engaging after you have given it some more thought, then write about it. If you're like most of my students (and me), you'll find that you come up with even better ideas after you get rolling. Now, let's figure out how to get rolling.

The suggestions in this chapter are geared toward the most common type of research paper assignment psychology undergraduates are likely to receive: a research literature review on a psychological topic. Exhibit 1.1 shows how the suggestions described in this chapter can be applied to other types of writing assignments, specifically, reaction papers and book reviews.

PRODUCTIVE BRAINSTORMING

You've heard about brainstorming since you were in elementary school, and it probably seems pointless. Brainstorming falls into the same category as lots of things your teachers or parents told you to do on faith, even when the benefits are not immediately obvious—eating vegetables, flossing, running for exercise. To a child, these habits seem pointless, but as an adult, it's obvious they improve your quality of life.

In the classic 1980s movie *The Karate Kid* (Weintraub & Avildsen, 1984), Daniel LaRusso moves from New Jersey to California because his mother changed jobs. Daniel doesn't want to move. He likes New Jersey and, sure enough, when he gets to California, he is bullied by disciples of a local karate dojo—the Cobra Kai. Despondent from his repeated beatings at the hands of the Cobra Kai, Daniel turns to the maintenance man at his apartment building, Mr. Miyagi, for karate lessons. Daniel shows up for his lessons assuming he'll learn roundhouse kicks, knockout punches, and other karate awesomeness. Instead, Miyagi asks him to clean and wax his cars, sand his deck, paint his fence, and paint his house.

Being asked to paint Miyagi's house is the last straw—Daniel freaks out and tells Miyagi that he wants to learn to defend himself, not to do Miyagi's

---

Exhibit 1.1

Principles of Brainstorming That Can Be Used for Any Assignment

The principles of brainstorming are the same regardless of the specific assignment. Indeed, the key principle is to clearly identify the task of the assignment, ask a question related to the task, and list potential responses to the question. Repeat the question and response cycle as needed. Examples of ways to get going for other assignments are as follows:

- Reaction paper: Suppose you're asked to write a reaction paper about your perspective on psychotherapy versus medication in the treatment of depression. Start brainstorming by considering the arguments for or against medication (or therapy). Review lecture materials or reading assignments about treatments. Did the book present reasons for or against a treatment? What were the reasons? Do you agree?
- Book review: Suppose you are asked to write a review of a book (either fiction or nonfiction) that is related to the topic of your class. Start brainstorming by thinking about your favorite parts of the book. What made them interesting? Evaluate the book from the perspective of the class. Were the ideas consistent with the scientific evidence presented in class?

Adjust these examples as needed to fit the specific task of your assignment.

---

housework. But then Miyagi shows Daniel that he has been learning how to defend himself all along using the repetitive motions he learned while working. Miyagi tries to punch Daniel and tells Daniel to do the hand and arm motion for "wax the car" as a means of self-defense. Daniel quickly learns that "wax the car," "sand the deck," "paint the fence," and "paint the house" are motions to block all manner of punches, kicks, and other attacks

Miyagi throws at him. So it is with brainstorming. As you brainstorm regularly, you will improve your ability to generate ideas.[1]

The point of brainstorming is to produce ideas. Lots of ideas. Good ones and bad ones. The biggest impediment to producing ideas is spending too much time analyzing and judging—letting your inner critic take control. When that happens, you are so worried about coming up with something good that you often come up with nothing at all. When you brainstorm, turn off your inner critic and just start writing down any idea at all, without worrying about how good it is. I find that dictating ideas on my smartphone can be a good way to keep my inner critic under control because I don't see the ideas in front of me on the screen as they are recorded. Regardless of the method, just start producing ideas for potential paper topics: How does sleep affect memory? What is the role of dreaming? How effective are treatments for marital problems? How does a brain injury affect impulsivity? How often, and under what circumstances, is the insanity defense successful?

Here are a few questions to ask yourself to help jump-start your brainstorming:

- What topics in psychology made you interested in the major?
- What behavior in your own life or in a friend or family member do you want to understand better? (This does not have to be an abnormal behavior. Perhaps your sister is particularly altruistic and you want to understand the psychology of altruism.)
- What was your favorite lecture in the class you are in or in your introductory psychology course?
- If your teacher has assigned a general topic—for example, you must write about cognitive psychology—what chapter from your textbook or lecture was the most interesting?

As you get going, you'll find that although some ideas may be worthless, others might be great. Later in this chapter, we'll discuss how to evaluate the merit of your ideas.

---

[1] I want to thank my colleague Scott Braithwaite for suggesting this connection between *The Karate Kid* and development of skills through regular, consistent practice.

USING MEDIA TO GENERATE IDEAS

If you're having trouble generating any ideas at all, try turning to popular media for inspiration. Think about your favorite movie or TV show—what makes the characters interesting, and why are you drawn to them? This could lead you to interesting psychological questions you can address in your paper. The following four examples illustrate how popular media can inspire topics for a research paper:

1. In the movie *Good Will Hunting* (Bender & Van Sant, 1997), the main character, Will, is a young adult who regularly gets arrested despite the fact that he is a genius and could easily move away from the difficult environment in which he lives. Will was an orphan who was abused in the various foster homes he was placed in. A paper could take a developmental psychology focus and examine the role of early home environment in later development, and especially in delinquency.

2. In the book and movie *The Fault in Our Stars* (Godfrey, Bowen, & Boone, 2014; Green, 2012), the main character, Hazel, is a 16-year-old girl with cancer. Not surprisingly, cancer has taken a toll on Hazel physically, requiring her to use an oxygen tank to help her breathe, as well as emotionally and socially. Consequently, her parents encourage her to attend a support group. *The Fault in Our Stars* is the story of a relationship Hazel develops after attending a support group meeting. A paper could take a health psychology focus and examine the efficacy of support groups in promoting the emotional health of cancer patients, or it could examine the role of social support in improving adherence to cancer treatment or coping with end-of-life issues.

3. The movie *Concussion* (Landesman et al., 2015) is the true story of Dr. Bennet Omalu and his quest to bring to light the health dangers professional football players face. Dr. Omalu discovers that some football players develop what he called chronic traumatic encephalopathy because of repeated blows to the head (even with a helmet on). The National Football League is not pleased with his findings and tries to discredit his work. This movie could inspire a number of papers. A paper could take a neuropsychology focus and examine the role of

sports in brain injuries or the impact of brain injuries on emotional and physical health. Another paper could take a social psychology focus and examine the role big corporations play in medical policy and other social issues.

4. The TV show *Monk* (Breckman & Hoberman, 2002–2009) is about a San Francisco–based detective, Adrian Monk, who is an exceptional detective but struggles with behaviors consistent with obsessive–compulsive disorder (OCD), such as a fear of germs and a need for order and symmetry. His obsessive behavior aids his work as a detective because it helps him focus on details at a crime scene others miss. However, his behavior also puts a strain on his relationships because he expects others to accommodate his fears. A paper could take an abnormal psychology focus and examine what factors lead to the development of OCD (i.e., why does it begin?), what factors maintain OCD (i.e., what keeps it around?), or even what OCD actually is and whether it's accurately represented in the media. A paper could also examine the impact of mental disorders on relationships.

These ideas are just the tip of the iceberg, both for the shows I mentioned and for the popular media generally. Authors spend a lot of time thinking about what makes their characters interesting—take advantage of that to get your paper off the ground.

STRATEGIES AFTER BRAINSTORMING

Now that you've spent some time brainstorming, you should have a list of ideas. The next step is to choose one idea and narrow it down to a manageable topic for your paper. Alternatively, if you've been assigned a general topic, your task now is to hone in on the specific subtopic you'd like to write about. For example, by reading about OCD, you can distinguish between the question "What are the treatments for OCD?" and the question "How effective is exposure and response prevention for treating OCD?" The former is giant, and you'll get overwhelmed writing about paper about it. The latter is focused and something you could tackle for a class.

My experience has been that it's difficult to narrow a big idea down to a manageable paper topic if you don't know enough about the subject. It's like trying to learn a new song on the guitar when you know only a few chords or maybe only that there are chords but you don't yet know how to play them.

When I was a graduate student, my graduate advisor, Will Shadish, and I met each week to discuss my research and plan the next steps. We devoted our early meetings to developing ideas for my master's thesis. After spending several months developing an idea, I had a concern: How was I ever going to be able to come up with the two additional paper ideas I would need to complete my degree? Furthermore, I planned to become a professor, and I was going to need to write papers for my entire career. Where would the ideas come from? Will's response to my concern was both motivating and humbling: "Scott, you don't know enough. Ideas spring from knowledge." Will then told me to start by reading all his published papers (well over 100 by the time I was a student). His logic was simple: If I could immerse myself in his research program, I would develop a deep understanding of what had been done, who the key theorists were, and where the holes were. Using his published articles gave me a defined pool of papers to read. I did not have to expend any energy figuring out which papers to read; I just grabbed a copy of his papers from his lab and got to work.

Your textbook can serve much the same purpose. The best way to learn enough to take a big idea and refine it to a manageable paper topic is to turn to your textbook. It likely contains all the information you need; all you have to do is read.

Suppose you're writing a paper for abnormal psychology. After brainstorming, you realize you're fascinated by OCD, and you'd like to write something about treatments for OCD. Start by reading the chapters on anxiety disorders, and try to understand how OCD fits within the broader diagnostic system. That is, what is OCD? What does the word *obsession* mean? Is it different from the way you would use the word with your friends? How does OCD develop? Is OCD different from other anxiety disorders? What implications might its differences have for treatment?

Once you have a handle on what OCD is, you can start to think about treatments more specifically. What kinds of treatments are listed as recommended for OCD? Have the treatments been studied? What distinguishes one kind of treatment from another? How many people might respond to the treatments? Keep asking questions and keep reading; as you do so, you'll better understand the topic and be able to distinguish between a huge topic you could write books about and one that is a manageable topic for a paper.

At times, your textbook won't provide all the answers you need. However, the references cited within your textbook likely will. Thus, you may need to start tracking down more sources to read. Look for review papers (i.e., papers that review portions of the literature); these will help you get perspective on the ideas. Eventually, you'll need to dive into the specific empirical studies; however, in the idea development stage, you're looking for the big picture, and review papers will be most helpful. Table 1.1 gives an example of using references from an abnormal psychology textbook (Butcher, Mineka, & Hooley, 2010) to start to learn about OCD and its treatment. In the reference list, you can find articles, book chapters, and books that provide more details. You don't want to write a paper that gives a general overview of OCD—the textbook already does that. Instead, you could use these references to deepen your understanding of OCD so that you can develop a specific, manageable idea for your paper.

Table 1.1

**Key References From an Abnormal Psychology Textbook[a]
That Provide Background Information for a Paper
on Treatments for Obsessive–Compulsive Disorder**

Authors	Reference type	Summary
What is OCD?		
Steketee & Barlow (2002)	Book chapter	Provides a more thorough overview of OCD than the textbook, including details about the disorder and discussion of treatment
Antony, Downie, & Swinson (1998)	Book chapter	Provides details about diagnostic issues in OCD, including categorizing the five main types of compulsions in OCD

Table 1.1

Key References From an Abnormal Psychology Textbook[a] That Provide Background Information for a Paper on Treatments for Obsessive–Compulsive Disorder (*Continued*)

Authors	Reference type	Summary
How does OCD develop?		
Mineka & Zinbarg (2006)	Review article	Contains a detailed discussion of behavioral theories regarding the development of anxiety disorders, including OCD
Rachman & Shafran (1998)	Book chapter	Describes cognitive and behavioral features of OCD; provides a behavioral understanding of how obsessions and compulsions are related
Enright & Beech (1993)	Article	Demonstrates that people meeting criteria for OCD struggle to ignore unwanted thoughts
What are the primary behavioral treatments for OCD?		
Franklin & Foa (2007)	Book chapter	Provides an overview of cognitive–behavioral treatments for OCD, with a special emphasis on exposure and response prevention (the most recommended treatment for OCD)
Franklin & Foa (2008)	Book chapter	Reviews cognitive–behavioral treatments for OCD; provides a brief treatment guide for the use of exposure and response prevention
What medications are used to treat OCD?		
Dougherty, Rauch, & Jenike (2007)	Book chapter	Reviews the literature on medications used to treat anxiety disorders, including OCD; includes information about relapse rates
Foa et al. (2005)	Article	Reports the results of a clinical trial comparing the effects of exposure and response prevention, medication, and a combination of both
Kushner et al. (2007)	Article	Examines whether a drug known as d-cycloserine, which is associated with fear, helps exposure treatment in OCD

Note. OCD = obsessive–compulsive disorder. [a]Butcher, Mineka, & Hooley, 2010.

SUMMARY

Coming up with an idea is a difficult part of writing. Fortunately, you have a number of tools at your disposal. Brainstorming is often one of the best ways to get going, if you can turn off your inner critic and just let the ideas flow. If you get stuck, you can use movie and other popular media to generate ideas. Popular media are rich with interesting characters and psychological questions. You can use your paper to examine the scientific basis (or lack thereof) of the psychology of the characters. Once you've chosen an idea, your textbook and other class materials will be particularly helpful in narrowing the idea down to a manageable topic for your research paper. Regardless of the specific method you use to develop a topic, if you put in the work to find an idea you care about, your paper will be better for it.

2

Finding Background Information and Literature

Once you've generated an idea and narrowed down your topic, it's time to start gathering sources that will provide the information you need to write your paper. Information isn't hard to find—searching the Internet and academic databases will produce endless amounts of information and potential sources. What can be difficult is sifting through this information to determine what is useful and appropriate and what isn't. No source is completely reliable; as illustrated in the examples that follow, even research published in scientific journals is sometimes discredited. Nonetheless, scientific journals are still your most reliable source, and other sources can also be reasonably reliable and appropriate. This chapter covers where to find information and gives tips for determining whether the information you find is appropriate for use in a scientific paper.

http://dx.doi.org/10.1037/0000045-003
Writing Your Psychology Research Paper, by S. A. Baldwin

THE CHALLENGE OF RECOGNIZING
FLIMSY SOURCES

It's important that your background information is accurate, thoughtful, and evidence based—in a word, rigorous. If the literature you use in your paper is fatally flawed or inaccurate, your paper will be too. Determining the quality of your sources can be difficult because nearly all sources, including books, journal articles, magazine stories, blog posts, and news stories, present information as the truth. However, many of these sources are not rigorous enough to be considered a scientific source or may simply present incorrect or inaccurate information. Sometimes identifying flimsy sources is easy, such as when a website advertises a new oil or pill that produces huge reductions in weight without changes in diet or exercise or when politicians make broad, sweeping claims about their opponents' positions.

However, at other times, recognizing flimsy data or claims can be challenging, especially when their source appears solid on the basis of where the data were published (e.g., a journal article that has been peer reviewed). This uncertainty makes scientific writing difficult because your task is not only to find evidence to support or contradict your thesis but also to evaluate and understand that evidence. To illustrate how challenging this can be, I describe two scientific studies that appeared and were cited as correct that turned out not to be accurate.

During the financial crisis that began in 2008, politicians, economists, and pundits argued long and hard about the best methods to promote economic growth. On one side of the debate, some argued for financial austerity, which means reducing government spending to ensure that the government doesn't take on additional debt. On the other side of the debate, some argued for government stimulus, which means increasing government spending to provide more money in the economic system (Krugman, 2013).

In 2010, two Harvard economists wrote an article titled "Growth in a Time of Debt" (Reinhart & Rogoff, 2010). In this article, the authors presented data to suggest that countries with debt greater than 90% of their gross domestic product (an indicator of the size of a nation's economy) had reduced economic growth compared with countries with less debt.

This paper was influential, and some politicians in the United States and Europe used it to argue for financial austerity as a means for improving the economy (Krugman, 2013; "The 90% Question," 2013).

Unfortunately, the analysis in Reinhart and Rogoff (2010) was influenced by an error in their Excel spreadsheet ("Influential Reinhart–Rogoff Economics Paper," 2013). When performing their calculations, they accidentally excluded data, which led to an underestimate of economic growth in countries with high debt and gross domestic product ratios. The degree of the underestimation is still a matter of debate (Coy, 2013), but it was an influential mistake that made it seem that austerity was the answer to the economic crisis, when in fact the answer continues to be unclear. Although Reinhart and Rogoff's miscalculation was highly influential, it appears that their mistake was unintentional.

Not all problems in the literature are honest mistakes. In 2014, Michael LaCour and Donald Green published a paper in *Science*, one of the most prominent journals in all of science, reporting on a study examining whether public opinion regarding same-sex marriage could be shifted by having gay people directly contact voters. The study compared whether voters' opinions changed after having visited with a gay or straight person about same-sex marriage. They reported that opinions changed regardless of the sexual orientation of the advocate but that the opinion change persisted only if voters had conversed with a gay advocate.

Their article gathered quite a bit of attention and was featured in *The New York Times*, *The Wall Street Journal*, and *This American Life* ("Author Retracts Study," 2015). Although this report had important implications politically as well as scientifically, the data were made up: LaCour had fabricated the data (Bohannon, 2015). Two graduate students at the University of California, Berkeley, David Brockman and Joshua Kalla, tried to replicate the findings and couldn't. They contacted LaCour's coauthor, Green, for some help. After Green was unable to get the necessary data and a satisfactory explanation from LaCour, Green requested that *Science* retract the paper (Bohannon, 2015). LaCour initially denied the claims but eventually admitted that he was not completely honest about the study ("Author Retracts Study," 2015). *Science* retracted the paper on May 28, 2015.

Exhibit 2.1

How to Find Useful Source Material

1. Look for scientific journals, and identify some of the primary journals in the field.
2. Distinguish between academic books and popular press books.
3. Use your university or college library, and talk with the librarian.
4. Distinguish between blog posts written by scientists and those that are not.
5. Use academic search engines.

So what does this mean for you? How can you tell which sources to use as material for your research paper? You may not always be able to tell on the basis of the information presented, whether a source is worthwhile. As the preceding examples illustrate, this is true for the scientific literature as well as the popular press (e.g., *The New York Times, The Huffington Post*) and purely online resources (e.g., Wikipedia). In the end, there are no fool-proof methods for ensuring that any given source is completely accurate and trustworthy. However, looking in the right places for source materials will increase the likelihood that what you find is sufficiently rigorous to be useful. Exhibit 2.1 lists tips for finding useful source material. Below, I elaborate on each tip.[1]

IDENTIFYING THE PRIMARY SCIENTIFIC JOURNALS IN THE FIELD

Your best source for background material will likely be scientific journals. A scientific journal is somewhat like a magazine in that it contains several articles written by different authors. Each article contains a description

---

[1] Your instructor may limit the kinds of sources you can use, such as to only journal articles. In that case, focus on those sources. However, it is still useful to think about why one kind of source may be more useful than another.

of scientific research and results. Articles vary in length and topic, but they are the primary outlet for scientists to share their research.

What makes scientific journals distinct from other sources is the process by which articles are selected for publication. This process is known as *peer review*. After researchers complete their study and write up their results, they submit the article to a journal to consider for publication. The editor of the journal sends the article to three or four researchers who can provide a careful review. These reviewers submit their critique to the editor and make a recommendation: reject, ask for revisions, or accept. The editor makes a decision and sends feedback to the authors. If the article is not rejected, then the authors typically make some revisions to their paper to address the reviewers' criticisms. The editor may then send the revised article out for further review or just make a decision based on the authors' revisions.

Although it is not perfect, the goal of peer review is to improve the rigor and quality of the scientific literature. Because scientists review other scientists' work, the conceptual and methodological flaws of that work should be caught during the review process. This means that articles in scientific journals are generally more reliable than those in other sources. It doesn't always work (see the examples above), but it is generally useful. Consequently, I strongly recommend that you prioritize peer-reviewed articles among your source material.

DISTINGUISHING BETWEEN ACADEMIC BOOKS AND POPULAR PRESS BOOKS

A second good source for background information is books, which tend to provide both an overview of a subject and a detailed look at some aspects of that subject. Ideally, the book as a whole presents a coherent narrative of a research area and then, within each chapter, dives deep into a specific topic. For example, one of my favorite books about psychotherapy research is *The Great Psychotherapy Debate* (Wampold & Imel, 2015). The primary question of this book has two parts: (a) How effective is psychotherapy, and (b) why is psychotherapy effective? Each chapter examines one of these questions by examining a specific topic in detail, such as the relative efficacy of different types of psychotherapy or the role of the therapist.

When searching for books on a topic, it is a good idea to distinguish between academic books and popular press books. *Academic books* are what I just described—books that discuss a major research topic (e.g., effects of psychotherapy, brain processes in memory). Academic books are typically aimed toward researchers and students for use in research and classes and are nearly always written by researchers. *Popular press books* are what make up the Psychology or Self-Help sections at a bookstore and, thus, are aimed toward the general public rather than researchers and students. Popular press books are written by lay authors, journalists, clinicians, and researchers. Although they cover a huge range of topics, popular press books tend not to be as grounded in research as academic books. This means that popular press books generally are not the best sources for your research paper.

If you search for books the way you are used to searching for anything else, (i.e., using Google or Amazon), popular press books are usually what you find first. An Amazon search is typically sorted by popularity, so even though Amazon carries both popular press and academic books, the results you see will likely be heavily skewed toward popular press books. The first page for a search on books about OCD on Amazon yielded the following sources:

- *The Mindfulness Workbook for OCD: A Guide to Overcoming Obsessions and Compulsions Using Mindfulness and Cognitive Behavioral Therapy* (Hershfield & Corboy, 2013)
- *Brain Lock: Free Yourself From Obsessive–Compulsive Disorder* (Schwartz & Beyette, 1997)
- *Freedom From Obsessive Compulsive Disorder* (Grayson, 2014)

These are all self-help, or popular press, books. The first academic book doesn't appear until the second page of results:

- *Obsessive–Compulsive Disorder in Adults* (Abramowitz & Jacoby, 2014)

Thus, I recommend not using Amazon or other bookstores to search for sources because you may find the wrong kinds of sources for a research paper.

Of course, popular press books aren't necessarily bad. Popular press books can be useful in your research by helping you generate ideas or providing some interesting stories to help give your paper a bit of color. However, they should rarely, if ever, be the foundation of your paper because they are written to sell rather than to review, evaluate, and extend a research area. Your best bet for finding quality academic books is your school's library.

USING YOUR UNIVERSITY OR COLLEGE LIBRARY AND LIBRARIAN

I've told you to focus your research on peer-reviewed articles and academic books. Next, we'll discuss the best ways to find these sources. The first place to look is your university's library, and the second place is the Internet using academic search engines.

I started college in 1996, graduate school in 2001, and my first job in 2006. Methods for finding and obtaining journal articles, books, and other source materials changed dramatically in those 10 years. When I started college, my freshman writing class required that each student take a tour of the library. As you can imagine, it wasn't exactly a popular assignment; however, it was necessary because the information we needed for our papers could be found only by going to the library. Any research paper began with hours spent hunting for articles and copying hundreds of pages of literature to haul back to my apartment for review.

Students still receive some library training, but most of it is web based and can be done from the comfort of their dorm rooms. Like my students, I rarely need to go to the library to do any of the research I need. My university's library website provides me access to many databases, electronic books, and electronic journals that I need. On the off chance I need a hard copy of a book or a journal article that the library doesn't have access to, I simply submit a request, and it is delivered to my office or e-mailed to me. It's awesome.

Although modern university libraries are remarkably convenient, if you don't spend time in the library or, at the very least, get to know the resources a library offers, you can miss out on useful information. For example, the library can provide you with training on how to effectively and efficiently search electronic databases. Unlike searching Google, you cannot simply type your question into the search bar. Instead, you must search using key words.

The library website at my university provides a tutorial on how to use key words to facilitate this search (Harold B. Lee Library, 2017). The website suggests four steps.

Suppose the topic for your paper is "The Effects of Treatments for Pediatric Obsessive–Compulsive Disorder." The first step is to identify the distinct words in your topic: *effects, treatments, pediatric, obsessive, compulsive,* and *disorder.* Second, you identify synonyms for the words. For example, possible synonyms or related words for *pediatric* are *child, childhood,* and *adolescent.* Possible synonyms for *treatments* are *interventions, medication,* and *psychotherapy.* Third, you truncate the key words (i.e., shorten them) to obtain all possible variations on each root word. Typically, you use an asterisk to represent the truncation—"treat*" expands to *treat* and *treatment,* for example. Fourth, you can group key words into phrases, putting each phrase in quotes, so the computer searches for the phrase rather than the key words separately. In this example, you would use the phrase "obsessive–compulsive disorder."

The tutorial also discusses how to improve searches using Boolean operators (Harold B. Lee Library, 2017). *Boolean operators* are words that denote logical relationships, and they typically are capitalized. In the case of key word searches, the three most prominent operators are *AND, OR,* and *NOT.* For example, if you want to limit your search only to psychotherapy and to exclude studies that involve medication, you could search as follows: (child* OR pediatric) AND (treat* OR psychotherapy) AND ("obsessive–compulsive disorder") NOT (medication) using parentheses to group the key words. In plain language, this search says, "Find articles involving the key word *child** or *pediatric* and the key word *treat** or *psychotherapy* and the phrase *obsessive–compulsive disorder,* but exclude articles with the key word *medication.*"

Once you have identified your key words and phrases and linked them with the appropriate Boolean operators, you can use them to search a database (see the discussion of commonly used academic search engines in the next section). Sometimes, even after following these steps, you may find that your searches produce too many possible references to be useful. Thus, you may need to narrow your search to produce more focused results (e.g., limiting the years you search or using more-specific key words). Librarians are particularly helpful when it comes to improving your key word searches.

Another useful tool most libraries have access to is the *Social Sciences Citation Index (SSCI)*, also known as the *Web of Science*. This citation index tracks the articles that cite a particular article. Most articles in an area cite major, foundational articles in that area. Consequently, if there is a seminal article in an area, you can search for the articles that have cited it. For example, a major clinical trial comparing psychotherapy and medication for pediatric OCD is the Pediatric OCD Treatment Study (POTS; POTS Team, 2004). Most studies evaluating pediatric OCD treatments cite the POTS trial. Thus, using the *SSCI* can help you identify treatment studies occurring after the POTS trial.

The top panel of Figure 2.1 shows the *SSCI* entry for the POTS trial. In addition to the bibliographic details for the POTS trial, the *SSCI* entry shows that as of January 2016, the POTS trial had been cited 285 times. Clicking on the "times cited" link produces the bottom panel of Figure 2.1, which provides bibliographic information for the 285 sources that cited the POTS trial. You can click on the title of each source to get additional details (e.g., the abstract). If your library has access to the articles, you can download pdf copies of the articles from within the *SSCI*.

I have only scratched the surface of what most libraries can offer. Although Google and other search engines are remarkably useful and a good first step in many research projects, the library exists to house and provide access to the resources that can deepen your research and to ensure that you have access to necessary information to write a great paper. Pay a visit to your library, and find out what services they offer to help with research papers. Sign up for that tour of the library. Before you

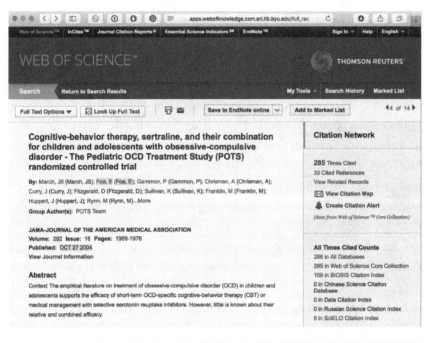

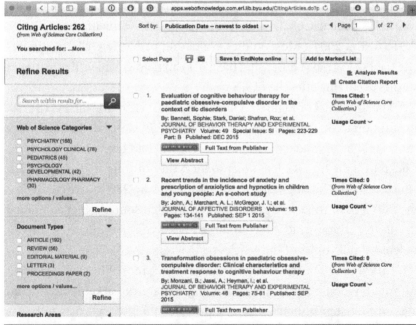

Figure 2.1

Example search from the *Social Sciences Citation Index*. The top panel shows the seminal source, and the bottom panel lists some of the articles that cited the seminal source. Thompson Reuters, the Thompson Reuters logo, and the Web of Science logo are registered trademarks of Thompson Reuters.

know it, you'll be good at searching for background material, and you might even enjoy it.

USING ACADEMIC SEARCH ENGINES

When performing searches based on the skills you learn at the library, you should use an academic search engine. Academic search engines focus your search on academic sources, mostly journals and books, related to your topic. The three most prominent academic search engines are Google Scholar, PubMed, and PsycINFO.

Google Scholar

Google Scholar (https://scholar.google.com) is an excellent place to start your searches. A Google Scholar search differs from a standard Google search in that the Google Scholar search is limited to the academic literature, filtering out popular press sources that may be less rigorous. Google Scholar is freely accessible to anyone with an Internet connection, and it allows you to save source information in a digital library as a means of organizing your searches. The top panel of Figure 2.2 provides an example of a Google Scholar entry. As you can see, entries in Google Scholar are organized by the title of the paper or book and include a summary of the source (i.e., abstract) when available. Each entry also includes a link to the citation information for the article or book, which includes most of the bibliographic information you will need when citing the entry. The entries also provide a link to other sources that have cited the specific entry. The reference in Figure 2.2 was cited by 770 other sources available on Google Scholar; clicking on the "cited by" link produces Google Scholar entries for all 770 sources.

PubMed

PubMed (https://www.ncbi.nlm.nih.gov/pubmed) is another free resource that is accessible to anyone with an Internet connection. PubMed organizes

Figure 2.2

Sample entries from Google Scholar (top), PubMed (middle), and PsycINFO (bottom). Google and the Google logo are registered trademarks of Google Inc.

the academic literature for parts of the medical, life, and social sciences. Whether PubMed is useful to you depends on the specific area of psychology you're planning to write about. PubMed is particularly useful for finding literature in clinical psychology, health psychology, and neuropsychology. Like Google Scholar, PubMed lets you create an account and save your search information. Entries in PubMed include bibliographic information needed to cite the article, a summary of the entry, and links to full-text copies of the article when available. The middle panel of Figure 2.2 provides an example of a PubMed entry.

PsycINFO

PsycINFO (http://www.apa.org/pubs/databases/psycinfo/) is a database specifically geared toward psychologists. It is not free to use, but it is likely that your university has a subscription to it (making it free to you). PsycINFO is typically accessed through a web service called EBSCO. EBSCO allows you to search multiple databases simultaneously, so you can combine a search of PsycINFO with Medline (similar to PubMed). This feature helps remove redundancy in your searches, which can be frustrating if you search each of the databases separately. Like the other databases, EBSCO allows you to create an account and save your search. Furthermore, because you access EBSCO through a university subscription, you can access many articles directly from the search as long as your university has a subscription to the journal. The bottom panel of Figure 2.2 provides an example of a PsycINFO entry.

DISTINGUISHING BETWEEN BLOG POSTS WRITTEN BY SCIENTISTS AND THOSE THAT ARE NOT

Blogs are ubiquitous, covering every topic imaginable, so they seem like a great source of information. However, blog posts vary widely in quality, meaning that you must distinguish between blog posts written by scientists and those that are not. If you choose to use blog posts as background material for your paper, look for blogs that specifically try to communicate scientific ideas. Be sure to read the About page for the blog to learn who is writing the posts. If you are writing your paper on OCD, check to see whether the blog is written by a researcher, a clinician, a journalist, a person dealing with OCD, or a layperson reflecting on an interesting behavioral phenomenon. Each may have interesting things to say, but you should carefully examine whether the author is making an argument supported by evidence or is just expressing an opinion. You should also examine whether any evidence offered is well documented and from reputable sources (e.g., peer-reviewed articles or academic books) before including it as background material in your paper.

It can be challenging to evaluate material on blogs, especially when it is written in scientific language. One needs only to watch infomercials about the latest diet pill, workout routine, or kitchen appliance to see that people use the appearance of science to lend credibility to their product or idea. A popular example of this challenge is the controversy surrounding the blog foodbabe.com, run by Vani Hari. Hari's aim, according to her website, is "to investigate what's really in your food" and to help the reader "break free from the hidden toxins in your food" (Food Babe, 2017). Posts on Hari's site list the ingredients of popular food products that, she claims, are toxic or poisonous.

A controversial post was titled "Why It's Time to Throw Out Your Microwave" (Food Babe, 2012; the original post has been taken down but has been archived). In this post, Hari argued that microwaves are harmful, citing peer-reviewed studies that she interpreted as indicating that microwaving vegetables reduces their antioxidant content. She also cited strange "evidence" that microwaving water has the same effects as speaking harmful words such as "Satan" or "Hitler" to the water—both the microwave and the harmful words, she alleged, prevent the water from forming beautiful crystals.

The evidence about crystal formation was easy enough to dismiss as implausible. Further, critics of Hari's claims pointed out that although the peer-reviewed study she cited concluded that microwaving vegetables does reduce antioxidants, the reduction was because the study authors added water when cooking vegetables in the microwave, and boiling vegetables on the stove has the same effect as boiling them in the microwave. The critics also cited numerous other studies showing the microwave to be effective and safe (Novella, 2014).

As shown in this example, simply citing a scientific study or two does not make a blog post scientific or evidence based. In order to make a claim about microwaves, OCD, memory, or childhood development, you need to review all the evidence relevant to the claim. Blog posts are not typically peer reviewed, and thus the author can make any number of claims and suggest that those claims are evidence based without being held accountable. Thus, use caution when considering blog posts as background information for your paper.

SUMMARY

The quality of your paper will be directly related to the quality of the literature you build your thesis on. We always have to trust, to at least a small degree, that the authors of our sources have described their data and their ideas rigorously and honestly. However, by prioritizing peer-reviewed articles and academic books, learning how to use your library's resources, searching for sources using academic databases, and being careful about blogs and other unreviewed sources, you can maximize the chances that your source material will be useful.

TWO

WRITING

3

Organizing Your Ideas and Creating a Thesis

Once you've gathered background information, the next step in writing a research paper is to organize and review the information you've gathered. This is a critical step to complete before you develop a thesis because without reviewing the literature, you won't know what your thesis is, and you'll have no idea where to begin. Every research paper needs a thesis, or main idea, and the paper should be structured so that all the other ideas in the paper are related to the thesis.

It's easy to get overwhelmed at this stage because the literature contains many different, and sometimes discrepant, ideas, and it can be challenging to distill them all into a coherent, useful thesis. This chapter gives you strategies for organizing the background information and then developing a thesis.

http://dx.doi.org/10.1037/0000045-004
Writing Your Psychology Research Paper, by S. A. Baldwin

SUMMARIZING ARTICLES

One of the best ways to begin organizing your background information is to summarize each article you've collected. Summarizing each article as you read through it will help you see the trends in the research you're reviewing. For example, you may see that one treatment consistently produces similar effects across many studies. You may also notice trends in the methodology (i.e., how a study is conducted) across many studies. These trends will help you determine how the literature you've gathered fits together and what the most important questions or topics may be.

Before you begin reading the materials you've gathered, create a short list of questions that you can use to summarize the highlights of each study. This step will give you a good starting point and ensure that you gather the same information from each article. I suggest that your summary cover at least the following questions:

- What was the primary question of the study?
  - State the primary question in your own words.
- What are the primary constructs or ideas involved in the study?
  - Identify the diagnosis, treatment, romantic relationships, brain development, genetics, methodology, and so forth examined in the study.
- What methods were used to study the question?
  - How many participants were in the study?
  - What kind of participants were they? For example, were the participants children, adults, or people with a condition (e.g., head injury)?
  - What kind of research design was used? Was the design experimental or observational? Was the design cross-sectional or longitudinal?
  - How were the key variables measured? Were the measures self-reports, observer ratings, biological measures, or something else? What are the names of the specific measurement tools?
- What were the results?
  - Summarize the results in one to two sentences. Most studies have many results and many analyses. Don't feel that you need to write them all down. Focus on the results that are most pertinent to the primary question.

- What were the limitations of the study?
  - Was the sample restricted (e.g., narrow age range)? Was the sample small? Did the researchers rely only on self-report measures? Was the design correlational when it could have been experimental? Was the experiment disconnected from the real world, and thus would the results not be likely to replicate in real life?

Exhibits 3.1, 3.2, and 3.3 provide three examples of study summaries using these questions.

GATHERING KEY QUOTES AND INFORMATION FROM SOURCES

Another useful method for organizing ideas is to identify key quotes from the literature. In addition to writing a brief summary for each source, I recommend that you find one quote that summarizes a key idea or finding from the articles you read. You will not necessarily use all the quotes in your paper, but they will help you develop and refine your thesis and other main ideas for your paper.

To illustrate, suppose your paper is on how cognitive therapy for depression works. As you read the background material, write down a key idea and supporting quote from each article you read. Don't worry too much about categorizing and comparing quotes from different articles at this point; just begin collecting them. Four ideas from the psychotherapy literature pertaining to the question of how cognitive therapy works, along with a supporting quote for each idea, are as follows:

1. Cognitive therapy is hypothesized to alter cognitive structures that cause and maintain depression:

   > Beck and his associates are quite specific about the hypothesized active ingredients of CT [cognitive therapy], stating throughout their treatment manual (Beck et al., 1979) that interventions aimed at cognitive structures or core schema are the active change mechanisms. Despite this conceptual clarity, the treatment is so multifaceted that a number of alternative accounts for its efficacy are possible.

Exhibit 3.1

Example Research Summary for a Psychophysiology Study

McNally, R. J., Lasko, N. B., Clancy, S. A., Macklin, M. L., Pitman, R. K., & Orr, S. P. (2004). Psychophysiological responding during script-driven imagery in people reporting abduction by space aliens. *Psychological Science, 15*, 493–497.

Can false memories produce intense emotions that are similar to true memories? That is, can memories of events that are improbable (e.g., abduction by aliens) produce the same kind of physiological response as memories of probable events (e.g., a car crash)? The key constructs in this study are memory of an improbable event, the degree to which the participant is prone to unusual ideas and ideation, and psychophysiological responding (e.g., heart rate).

The study was observational because there was no manipulation. The study included 10 people who believed they had been abducted by aliens and 12 people who served as controls. Each participant listened to a description of their abduction (or, if in the control condition, one of the abductee's descriptions) as well as a description of a stressful event, a positive event, and a neutral event. The dependent variables were heart rate, skin conductance, and electromyogram of the left frontalis facial muscle.

Self-identified abductees had a greater response on all three dependent variables than control participants for the abduction and stressful scripts but not for the positive and neutral scripts. Self-identified abductees did not respond more to the abduction script than the stressful script.

The study is limited by the small sample size. Because the abduction participants did not have a greater response to the abduction scripts than the stressful scripts, it is possible that the abduction participants are simply more reactive to unusual stimuli than controls.

Exhibit 3.2

Example Research Summary for a Treatment Study

Jacobsen, N. S., Dobson, K. S., Truax, P. A., Addis, M. E., Koerner, K.,
Gollan, J. K., . . . Prince, S. E. (1996). A component analysis of cognitive-
behavioral treatment for depression. *Journal of Consulting and Clinical
Psychology, 64,* 295–304.

What are the mechanisms of change in cognitive–behavioral treatment for depression? Do they include behavioral activation (i.e.,
getting engaged in life again)? Learning to cope with the negative
thoughts associated with depression? Changing the core ideas or
assumptions people have about themselves (i.e., changing core
schemas)?

The authors divided cognitive–behavioral therapy into its component parts to see which part produced the most change in depressive symptoms. Participants were randomly assigned to receive one
of three treatments. The treatments represented one or more of the
component parts of cognitive–behavioral therapy: (a) behavioral
activation; (b) behavioral activation plus skills to cope with negative
thoughts; and (c) behavioral activation, coping skills, and focus on
core schema. In addition to the treatments, the key construct in this
study is depression.

The study was experimental. The sample included 152 participants
who met criteria for major depression. The primary outcomes
measures were the Hamilton Rating Scale for Depression, which
is rated by a clinician (not the therapist), and the Beck Depression
Inventory, which is self-report. After 20 sessions of treatment, all
treatments showed an effect on depressive symptoms, but the treatments did not differ from one another. This was true immediately
after treatment and at the 6-month follow-up.

There were no major limitations. Sample sizes were relatively
large, and dropout from treatment was fairly small (less than 10%).

Exhibit 3.3

Example Research Summary for a Correlational Study

Creed, T. A., & Kendall, P. C. (2005). Therapist alliance-building behavior within a cognitive–behavioral treatment for anxiety in youth. *Journal of Consulting and Clinical Psychology, 73*, 498–505.

The *therapeutic alliance* refers to the relationship between a therapist and client. The alliance includes the emotional bond between therapist and client as well as the degree to which they agree on goals and the interventions used to meet those goals. The study aimed to understand what therapist behaviors predict high ratings of the alliance in cognitive–behavioral therapy for youth. The key construct in this study is the therapeutic alliance.

The study was observational. The study included 56 children who received 16 sessions of cognitive–behavioral therapy. The alliance was measured by the Therapeutic Alliance Scale for Children, which was rated by both the child and the therapist. Therapist behaviors thought to be related to the alliance were rated by the Therapist Alliance-Building Behavior Scale. The therapist behaviors were coded by graduate students in clinical psychology.

Collaboration between therapist and patient predicted higher ratings of the alliance, whereas pushing the child to talk, emphasizing common ground, and being overly formal predicted lower ratings of the alliance.

The study is limited by its sample size. Although not a tiny study, 56 children may not be enough to produce stable results given the number of predictors they examined. The study is also limited by the fact that only one kind of treatment (cognitive–behavioral therapy) was used.

We label two primary competing hypotheses the "activation hypothesis" and the "coping skills" hypothesis. (Jacobson et al., 1996, p. 295)

2. A treatment can affect cognitive variables either directly or indirectly:

A treatment need not directly cause change in the presumed mediator to have a causal impact on that mediator. That is, indirect paths, such as one that runs from treatment through depression to cognition, are every bit as viable as a direct path from treatment to cognition. This indirect path requires nothing more than that changes in depression produce changes in cognition, that is, that cognitive processes be, at least in part, state-dependent consequences of the clinical phenomenon of depression. (Hollon, DeRubeis, & Evans, 1987, p. 143)

3. Therapist adherence to treatment protocols is not correlated with outcomes:

In this systematic review, we analyzed findings from 36 studies in which therapist adherence or competence was examined in relation to outcome. The most striking result is that variability in neither adherence nor competence was found to be related to patient outcome and indeed that the aggregate estimates of their effects were very close to zero. One explanation for these results is that adherence and competence are relatively inert therapeutic ingredients that play at most a small role in determining the extent of symptom change. It is possible that the constituent studies in which significant positive adherence–outcome and competence–outcome effect sizes were reported were simply chance findings from a population in which variability in adherence and competence accounts for little, if any, variability in outcome. (Webb, DeRubeis, & Barber, 2010, p. 207)

4. Cognitive therapy helps prevent relapse of depressive symptoms, indicating that cognitive therapy may help patients learn how to cope with depression:

The findings of this study suggest that CT [cognitive therapy] has an enduring effect that reduces risk following successful treatment, as indicated by the reduced relapse rates relative to medication withdrawal. Moreover, the magnitude of the CT effect seems to be at least as great as that achieved by keeping patients on continuation medication, which is widely regarded as the most effective means of preventing relapse. Thus, it seems that there are at least 2 ways to protect patients against relapse following successful treatment: to either continue ADM [antidepressant medication] or provide CT during acute treatment. Moreover, there are indications that the enduring effect of CT may extend to the prevention of recurrence. (Hollon et al., 2005, p. 421)

STRUCTURING YOUR PAPER

Again, the purpose of collecting the quotes is not to have lots of quotes to use in your paper. Instead, the quotes are there to help you remember the most important ideas in the literature you've gathered and to make it easier for you to decide what the main ideas of your paper should be. Look through your article summaries and key quotes, and begin to sort them into main ideas. You may even want to print out the key quotes and summaries and cut them apart so you can physically sort them.

For instance, the four ideas and quotes listed above could lead you to decide that one part of your paper could be a review of the mechanisms by which cognitive therapy is hypothesized to work—sometimes referred to as the *mechanisms of change*. A second part of your paper could discuss ways in which the evidence supports or contradicts the proposed mechanisms of change. A third part of your paper could discuss evidence for and against the proposed mechanisms of change, which would combine Ideas 3 and 4 listed above. Figuring out what each section of your paper could cover will help you determine your main idea, or thesis statement.

Thesis Statement

The foundation of your paper is your thesis statement. A thesis isn't the same thing as the topic of your paper. The topic of your paper is a general idea or content area and is often stated in the form of a question. For example, the topic of my example paper is, How does cognitive therapy for depression work? The thesis, on the other hand, is a claim or statement *about* the topic of your paper. For example, your thesis statement could be a claim about how cognitive therapy works: "Although evidence suggests that cognitive therapy is an effective treatment for depression, the evidence for why cognitive therapy works is limited and not consistent with the hypothesized mechanisms."

As I noted at the beginning of this chapter, this is not an idea I could have come up with before studying the literature. What I had before I studied the literature was simply a topic (i.e., cognitive therapy). After studying the literature, I am able to make a statement or claim about my topic (i.e., how cognitive therapy works). In my experience as a teacher, students often forget to formulate a thesis for their paper and simply focus on a topic. Consequently, their papers are not sufficiently focused. Instead, they meander through lots of studies and ideas that are related to a topic but are not tightly related to one another, making it difficult to see how the specific ideas are connected. If you have a thesis statement, however, then each study you discuss and each new idea you introduce can provide evidence for or against your thesis.

Having a thesis statement also makes it easier to weed through the background information you've collected: You don't have to use every bit of information you've collected in your paper. Sort your article summaries and key quotes into three or four groups on similar themes. As you get to the next step—outlining—you'll determine which ones are pertinent (keep these) and which ones are extraneous (set these aside).

Outline

Once you have a thesis statement and ideas for a few sections that will support the thesis, you are ready to start outlining. Outlines are useful at this stage of writing. An outline gives you structure, which will require you to consider the logic and flow of your paper. At the same time, an outline is flexible enough to allow you to try out ideas and see whether the ideas make sense in the context of your paper without your writing entire pages only to find out that the material does not fit well within your paper. Although there isn't only one correct way to outline, Exhibit 3.4 illustrates one way to use outlines that has worked well in my writing.

Outlining a research paper is often a two-step process. The first step is to use an outline to organize the information you've gathered. The second step is to fit that information into the accepted structure of a research

---

Exhibit 3.4

An Example Outline for a Paper on the Topic of Cognitive Therapy for Depression

I. Introduction
   A. Define *depression*
      1. Diagnostic definition (American Psychiatric Association, 2013; textbook)
      2. Case example
   B. Discuss possible treatments for depression
     Look in textbook for definitions of treatments. Given that we have discussed cognitive therapy a lot in class, I feel pretty good about explaining cognitive therapy. I'm less confident about interpersonal therapy, so I will need to look that material up.
      1. Cognitive therapy
      2. Interpersonal therapy
      3. Medications
   C. Briefly review the evidence for cognitive therapy
     My textbook covers this, but I will need to get some of the original studies and review articles.
      1. How does cognitive therapy compare to no treatment (Dobson, 1989)?
      2. How does cognitive therapy compare to other psychotherapy?
      3. How does cognitive therapy compare to medication (Hollon, DeRubeis, & Evans, 1987; Hollon et al., 2005)?

Exhibit 3.4

**An Example Outline for a Paper on the Topic
of Cognitive Therapy for Depression (*Continued*)**

    D. Purpose of this paper

        1. Thesis: *Although there is good evidence that cognitive therapy is an effective treatment for depression, the evidence for why cognitive therapy works is limited and not consistent with the hypothesized mechanisms.* This is my working draft of my thesis. Still working through the literature and trying to understand it.

  II. How cognitive therapy is proposed to work

    A. Cognitive therapy → cognitive variables → treatment outcome (Hollon et al., 1987)

    B. Discuss the cognitive variables (Beck, Rush, Shaw, & Emery, 1979)

        1. Automatic thoughts

        2. Thinking errors

        3. Schemas

    C. Discuss the parts of cognitive therapy (Beck et al., 1979)

        1. Behavioral activation

        2. Challenging thoughts

        3. Schema work

    D. Possible mechanisms for cognitive therapy (Jacobson et al., 1996)

        1. Coping skills vs. activation hypothesis

        2. See the quote from Jacobson et al. (1996)

 III. Methods and models for evaluating the mechanisms of change

    A. Hollon et al.'s (1987) models

        They use a lot of technical terms. Will likely need to translate. Weakest part of the outline for sure. Needs work. Also,

(continues)

Exhibit 3.4

An Example Outline for a Paper on the Topic of Cognitive Therapy for Depression (*Continued*)

if I am going to use this, I will need to organize the evidence studies for these categories.

    1. Causal specificity/consequential specificity

    2. Noncausal nonspecificity/consequential nonspecificity

    3. Causal nonspecificity/consequential nonspecificity

    4. Causal specificity/consequential nonspecificity

    5. Noncausal nonspecificity/consequential specificity

IV. Evidence

    A. Adherence to treatment protocols is not strongly related to outcome (Webb, DeRubeis, & Barber, 2010).

        1. The specific techniques therapists use in cognitive therapy may not be related to change.

    B. Both cognitive therapy and medication can produce change in cognitive variables (Simons, Garfield, & Murphy, 1984).

        1. Cognitive change may follow change in depression rather than precede change in depression.

    C. Relapse rates are lower for cognitive therapy than medication once treatment is discontinued (Hollon et al., 2005).

        1. Something unique may be learned in cognitive therapy.

V. Conclusion

    A. Need to sort out the rest of the paper and then start brainstorming

    B. To be determined

paper (covered in Chapter 4). For now, start creating an outline that shows how the information you've gathered fits together. After sorting your summaries and key quotes into three or four different groups, make a heading for each group, and summarize that group's main idea. Then, under each heading, list more specific ideas or evidence supporting the main idea. Go through every summary and key quote and see where it fits in your outline.

When outlining, it can be useful to remember that the *Publication Manual of the American Psychological Association* (APA) can help you organize the structure of your paper (APA, 2009, pp. 62–63). APA Style includes multiple headings that orient readers to the sections of a paper. The headings are ordered hierarchically, with the top-level heading, Heading 1, being centered on the page and bold. Heading 2 is flush left and bold. Heading 3 is bold and followed by a period. Exhibit 3.5 illustrates the heading styles. I like to think of the parts of my outlines as corresponding to the headings in APA Style. That is, levels of my outline preceded by a Roman numeral correspond to Heading 1, outline levels preceded by a capital letter correspond to Heading 2, and outline levels preceded by a number correspond to Heading 3. This strategy helps me visualize the paper as I outline. It also helps me rein in the number of parts I add to my outline—if I have too many top-level ideas, I'm trying to do too much, and my paper is going to muddled and confusing.

Exhibit 3.4 is an outline that organizes research on my paper topic, cognitive therapy. It begins with an introduction that includes a definition of depression and background information relating to different

---

Exhibit 3.5

Heading Formats in APA Style

Heading 1

Heading 2

    Heading 3. A major depressive episode can include low mood, loss of interest or pleasure, suicidal ideation, concentration difficulties, . . .

treatments for depression. The introduction also includes my thesis statement about how cognitive therapy works.

After the introduction to the concepts in my paper and my thesis statement in Section I, there are three main sections. Each of these sections pertains directly to the thesis statement. Section I introduces the concepts in my paper and my thesis statement. Section II provides foundational definitions of the parts of cognitive therapy and hypothesized cognitive variables believed to be implicated in change. Section III does not explicitly review evidence of how cognitive therapy works, but it relates directly to my thesis by providing a foundational discussion of how researchers evaluate treatment mechanisms. Section IV reviews evidence about the mechanisms of change in cognitive therapy. Therefore, each part of the paper either (a) directly presents evidence about how cognitive therapy works or (b) provides the needed foundation for a clear understanding of the treatment mechanism studies.

Creating an outline makes it easy to tell whether you have enough background information and whether the information you've gathered is sufficiently focused on your thesis. If, as you outline, you realize that one of your main sections doesn't directly relate to your thesis, that most likely means you should cut that section from your paper. If you find that you have only one or two sections, you may need to do additional research or see whether those sections can be further broken down into different ideas (you're looking for three to four main ideas [sections] that all support your thesis). Additionally, an outline makes it easy to see where there may be holes in your background information—if two sections have lots of supporting information and the third section has hardly any at all, you'll be able to tell what specific information you should be looking for at this point.

Your outline should also include a conclusion. You may not know what you're going to say in your conclusion at this point, and that's OK. Just keep the heading there to remind yourself that you'll need to summarize and wrap up ideas at the end of your paper.

As you outline, keep in mind that the outline is not the finished product; the paper is. The outline should support your writing and assist you. It can be easy to get caught up in whether your outline is detailed enough or too long. Try to anticipate the major sections of your paper and consider how your ideas for the sections relate to your thesis and how each section relates to others. If it helps you to write more details, write them. Make this process useful to you. I've found that the less I know about a subject before writing a paper, the more detailed and thorough my outlines need to be. However, if I'm already familiar with a topic, outlines can be more like six to 12 bullet points. To start, I recommend that you develop an outline at the same level of detail and scope as Exhibit 3.4 for most class assignments (e.g., a 10-page research paper). If you're writing a more involved paper, such a senior thesis, you'll likely need to expand the scope or have a separate outline for each section of your paper.

Mind Map

If you get stuck while creating your outline, or just can't figure out what information should go where, you may want to try mind mapping. *Mind maps* are drawings that show connections between ideas. Ideas are typically written in circles, called *nodes*, and nodes are connected to one another with lines. The connections and nodes thus provide a visual representation of the main ideas of the paper and how they are connected. Given that you simply draw circles and connect them to one another, mind maps can be a bit more unstructured than outlines.

When I feel stuck with an outline and not sure where to go, I like to use a mind map as a brainstorming tool (see Chapter 1) to help generate ideas and look for areas I need to do more thinking or reading about. Seeing a node that is not connected to any main idea can indicate that the idea in the unconnected node may be extraneous and should be excluded from the paper. Figure 3.1 illustrates a mind map created with the same content as the outline in Exhibit 3.4. Although this mind map is structured and organized just like the outline, don't feel you need to create an outline when you use a mind map—formal organization can come later. The key is to visualize the content of your paper and see how the ideas are connected.

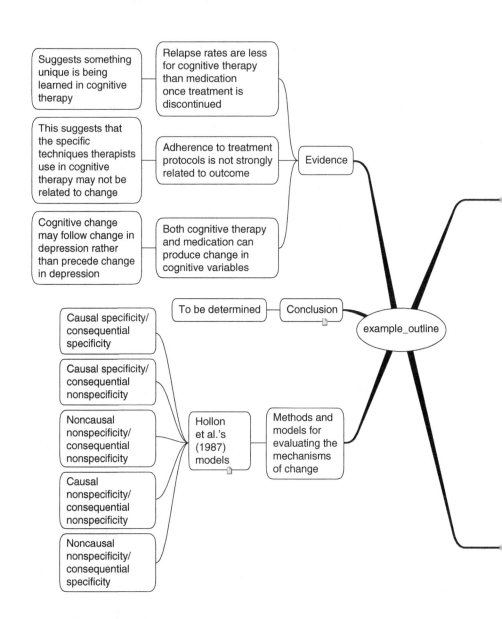

Figure 3.1

Example mindmap.

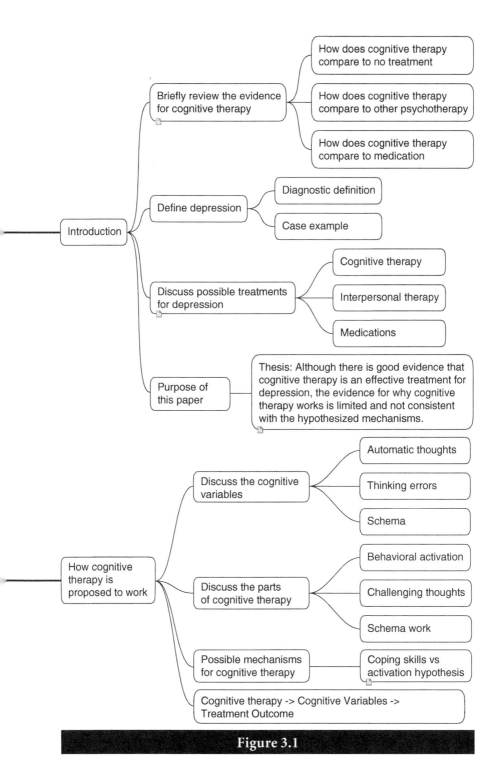

Figure 3.1

Example mindmap. (*Continued*)

SUMMARY

I've never regretted the time I've spent organizing, summarizing, outlining, and mind mapping before drafting my papers. It has never made writing harder or slowed me down so much that I've not been able to get my work done or meet deadlines. Rather, it helps me streamline the actual writing process and usually speeds things up. Furthermore, spending the time to get organized helps me feel more confident in my ideas because I've spent the time to understand and evaluate the literature. It's not difficult to recognize when I (or my students) have not spent the time to organize my thoughts and my background material because my writing tends to be less coherent and clear. Given that the point of writing is to communicate, it is well worth devoting time to the aspects of writing that improve communication.

4

Structuring and Drafting Your Paper

Once you've organized all your background material, it's nearly time to start drafting your paper. However, before you begin writing, you need to understand the explicit structure of a scientific paper so you'll be able to follow it as you write. This is the second step of outlining mentioned in Chapter 3. This chapter begins with a review of the accepted structure of a scientific research paper and then reviews guidelines for drafting your paper.

STRUCTURE OF A RESEARCH PAPER

Think about a movie you've seen recently that told an interesting story. Did you have to work hard to understand how events in the movie were connected? Did you get lost trying to understand who the characters were and what the scene had to do with the main plot? Probably not. Most

http://dx.doi.org/10.1037/0000045-005
Writing Your Psychology Research Paper, by S. A. Baldwin

movies do a pretty good job telling a story, and good storytelling is *coherent*, meaning it's easy to follow. Good writing is, at its heart, good storytelling. This means that good writing is coherent and logical and, again, easy to follow.

Good storytelling isn't limited to fiction; scientific writing also requires a narrative and an appropriate structure to help readers understand the story it tells. That is, readers need to be able to focus on understanding the content of your paper, such as the details of the research procedures, results of the experiment, or implications of the findings. If readers have to expend effort to understand how content fits together or to distinguish between existing and new findings, they will have less capacity to understand the ideas of the paper.

Fiction writing has a structure we're all familiar with. Chapters separate major scenes and plot moments. Scenes establish which characters are present, where the action takes place, and when the action happens. Scenes also set up the next bit of action in the book, such as introducing a problem a character must solve. With the exception of chapters, most fiction writing does not have an explicit structure—that is, written headings or sections that distinguish one part of the book from another.

Nonfiction writing, especially scientific writing, does have an explicit structure, which makes it predictable and easy to follow (and following the structure also makes it easier to write). A common way to think of the structure of a research paper is as two connected triangles or funnels. Figure 4.1 illustrates this. The beginning of the paper, corresponding to the widest part at the top of Figure 4.1, provides the broad context for your research question. For example, the paper I outlined in Chapter 3 is focused on reviewing why cognitive therapy for depression works. It begins with a brief review of depression and possible treatments for depression.

As you move down Figure 4.1, the triangle gets narrower, which corresponds to a narrower focus on the primary research question—the outline changes to a focus on cognitive therapy for depression specifically. The middle of Figure 4.1 is the narrowest, representing the focus of the paper. In my case, the narrow portion represents the thesis statement and purpose of the paper. The narrow portion also represents the methods used for addressing the research question and the results of the literature

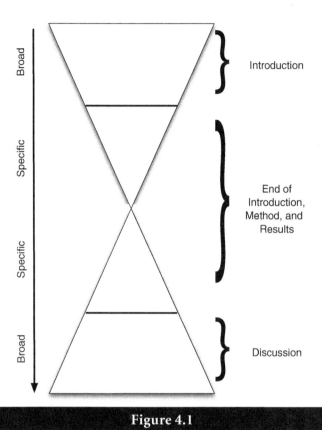

Figure 4.1

Example structure of a research paper.

review. In my outline, this corresponds to the discussion of how cognitive therapy is proposed to work, the methods and models for evaluating cognitive therapy, and the evidence for how cognitive therapy works.

Finally, the bottom of Figure 4.1 is wide. This is the section of the paper that connects the specific ideas generated in the paper back to the broader context. For example, I could reconnect the results of research on the mechanisms of change in cognitive therapy to other mechanism research in psychotherapy.

You can see in Figure 4.1 that the broad and specific areas of the paper correspond to the named sections. In psychology, nearly all research papers have four main sections: Introduction, Method, Results, and Discussion.

Each section has a specific purpose or role within the paper. Furthermore, given that most research papers include these specific sections, you don't need to create the broad structure of your paper from scratch, and your readers can predict what will be in each part.[1] Indeed, you can take your outline and place each part of the outline within the appropriate section (see Exhibit 4.1). If you find that an idea in your outline doesn't fit well with the structure, then you may need to consider revising the idea or dropping it. For example, Section D in the Results section in Exhibit 4.1 may be too tangential to the thesis, especially if there are strict page limits on the paper.

Introduction

The Introduction is the beginning of your paper and sets the context. The length of the Introduction varies by research area and subdiscipline norms. In clinical psychology, in which I publish regularly, Introductions range from three to seven pages, but if you're assigned a 10-page paper, your Introduction will probably be about one page long. In the Introduction, you'll include general background for your topic, evidence for why the topic is important, and the specific thesis statement you will address in the paper. Consistent with Figure 4.1, the content of the Introduction goes from broad to specific.

Begin the Introduction with a statement of your problem (e.g., pediatric obsessive–compulsive disorder [OCD], brain structures involved in memory). You shouldn't start the Introduction by just saying, "My paper is on how obsessive–compulsive disorder is treated in children." The title of your paper will make that clear. Instead, start by teaching about OCD, such as by briefly reviewing symptoms of OCD and how OCD manifests in children. If your paper is on memory, you could start by distinguishing between different types of memory (e.g., episodic memory) and giving examples of each. Although some readers may be experts in the topic of

---

[1] The ideas behind Figure 4.1 as well as many of the ideas in the rest of this chapter are based on materials from a course taught by Will Shadish, including the ideas on how to develop the Introduction, Method, Results, and Discussion sections and the example paragraphs about divorce and depression. I'd like to thank him for sharing his course notes with me and letting me use and adapt them here.

Exhibit 4.1

An Example Outline for a Paper on the Topic of Cognitive Therapy for Depression Including the Introduction, Method, Results, and Discussion Sections

I. Introduction

    A. Define *depression*

        1. Diagnostic definition (American Psychiatric Association, 2013; textbook)

        2. Case example

    B. Discuss possible treatments for depression

        Look in textbook for definitions of treatments. Given that we have discussed cognitive therapy a lot in class, I feel pretty good about explaining cognitive therapy. I'm less confident about interpersonal therapy, so I will need to look that material up.

        1. Cognitive therapy

        2. Interpersonal therapy

        3. Medications

    C. Briefly review the evidence for cognitive therapy

        My textbook covers this, but I will need to get some of the original studies and review articles.

        1. How does cognitive therapy compare to no treatment (Dobson, 1989)?

        2. How does cognitive therapy compare to other psychotherapy?

        3. How does cognitive therapy compare to medication (Hollon, DeRubeis, & Evans, 1987; Hollon et al., 2005)?

    D. Purpose of this paper

        1. Thesis: *Although there is good evidence that cognitive therapy is an effective treatment for depression, the evidence for why cognitive therapy works is limited and not consistent with the hypothesized mechanisms.* This is my working draft of my thesis. Still working through the literature and trying to understand it.

(continues)

Exhibit 4.1

An Example Outline for a Paper on the Topic of Cognitive Therapy for Depression Including the Introduction, Method, Results, and Discussion Sections (*Continued*)

II. Method
  A. Search procedures
    1. Search terms
    2. Databases
    3. Inclusion and exclusion criteria
  B. Flow chart for search
III. Results
  A. How cognitive therapy is proposed to work
    1. Cognitive therapy → cognitive variables → treatment outcome (Hollon et al., 1987)
    2. Discuss the cognitive variables (Beck, Rush, Shaw, & Emery, 1979)
      a. Automatic thoughts
      b. Thinking errors
      c. Schemas
  B. Discuss the parts of cognitive therapy (Beck et al., 1979)
    1. Behavioral activation
    2. Challenging thoughts
    3. Schema work
  C. Possible mechanisms for cognitive therapy (Jacobson et al., 1996)
    1. Coping skills vs. activation hypothesis
    2. See the quote from Jacobson et al. (1996)
  D. Methods and models for evaluating the mechanisms of change
    1. Hollon et al.'s (1987) models
      They use a lot of technical terms. Will likely need to translate. Weakest part of the outline for sure. Needs work. Also, if I am going to use this, I will need to organize the evidence studies for these categories.

> ## Exhibit 4.1
>
> **An Example Outline for a Paper on the Topic of Cognitive Therapy for Depression Including the Introduction, Method, Results, and Discussion Sections (*Continued*)**
>
>   a. Causal specificity/consequential specificity
>
>   b. Noncausal nonspecificity/consequential nonspecificity
>
>   c. Causal nonspecificity/consequential nonspecificity
>
>   d. Causal specificity/consequential nonspecificity
>
>   e. Noncausal nonspecificity/consequential specificity
>
>   E. Evidence
>
>   1. Adherence to treatment protocols is not strongly related to outcome (Webb, DeRubeis, & Barber, 2010).
>
>   a. The specific techniques therapists use in cognitive therapy may not be related to change.
>
>   F. Both cognitive therapy and medication can produce change in cognitive variables (Simons, Garfield, & Murphy, 1984).
>
>   1. Cognitive change may follow change in depression rather than precede change in depression.
>
>   G. Relapse rates are lower for cognitive therapy than medication once treatment is discontinued (Hollon et al., 2005).
>
>   1. Something unique may be learned in cognitive therapy.
>
> IV. Discussion
>
>   A. Summarize the primary conclusions
>
>   B. How results are connected to literature on mechanisms of change in all of psychotherapy
>
>   1. Lack of consistent evidence regarding change mechanisms
>
>   2. Common vs. specific factors
>
>   C. Limitations
>
>   1. Small number of studies
>
>   2. Generally small number of patients and therapists in each study

your paper, most will not. Thus, it is critical to provide a sufficiently general introduction to orient your readers.

After introducing the topic, make a case for why it is important. It might be important for public health reasons, practical reasons, or theoretical reasons. For example, you could find data on the public health impact of pediatric OCD—the number of children affected each year or the cost of untreated OCD. In the case of understanding why cognitive therapy works, you could tie the importance of understanding why a treatment works to improving the training and development of therapists. Or if your paper is about the brain and memory, you could make the case that to better understand how memory works at a theoretical level, a review and synthesis of brain-based models of memory are warranted.

You are now getting to the narrow portion of Figure 4.1. You've set the stage and made a case for why your topic is important. Now provide your thesis statement. What specific aspect of pediatric OCD, cognitive therapy for depression, or memory are you going to examine in your paper, and what claim are you going to make? You can't say everything that is interesting or important on the treatment of pediatric OCD, so you need to narrow it down. You might focus on the effects of medications on OCD symptoms or maybe even relapse rates of children treated with medications. This is the thesis or focus of the paper. If you've done the work and followed the steps discussed in previous chapters, this part of the Introduction should essentially write itself. Given that you've studied the background literature, it may be obvious to you why your specific question is interesting or important. Don't assume this is true for your reader; provide evidence and argue for why your specific question or claim is important.

Method

The Method section describes how you addressed your specific question. The primary aim of the Method section is to provide a clear, concise, and transparent description of the procedures you used so that another scholar could follow the same steps and replicate your work. The details of the Method section will depend on what kind of paper you write. If your paper is a literature review, such as the one outlined in Chapter 3, then the Method section should provide details about your search procedures. If your paper reports original data, such as an experiment or survey in a research design class, then the Method section should provide details about the participants, experimental manipulation, and measures you used.

Reporting on search procedures is simple. Describe the databases and search terms you used (see Chapter 2). Indicate how many articles the search suggested, and if you had to narrow your search, how you did so (e.g., removing specific search terms, putting a limit on publication date). I published a literature review known as a *meta-analysis* examining the effects of four types of family therapy for adolescent delinquency and substance abuse problems (Baldwin, Christian, Berkeljon, & Shadish, 2012). In that article, we described my search as follows:

> We identified studies by performing an electronic search on PsycINFO, Medline, and *Dissertation Abstracts International* for randomized trials published by February 2009. We used the following search terms: Multisystemic Therapy or Functional Family Therapy or Multidimensional Therapy or Brief Strategic Family Therapy or Family Therapy AND delinquency or delinquent or substance use or conduct disorder or externalizing. Additionally, we searched reference lists of previous reviews or studies of the four family therapies and the websites of the developers of the four family therapies. Eligible studies were examined by two reviewers. Any disagreements were settled by consensus. (Baldwin et al., 2012, p. 286)

As you can see in the quote, the specific form and structure of a Boolean search may vary across search engines. I recommend spending some time learning the requirements and conventions for the search engines you choose.

In addition to describing our search, we also included Figure 4.2, which depicts how many articles we located and why we excluded articles. These flow charts increase transparency in literature reviews—along with the text, they describe how and why you included or excluded articles from your review. In other words, they help protect authors from criticisms that they excluded studies simply because the studies did not have results consistent with their thesis.

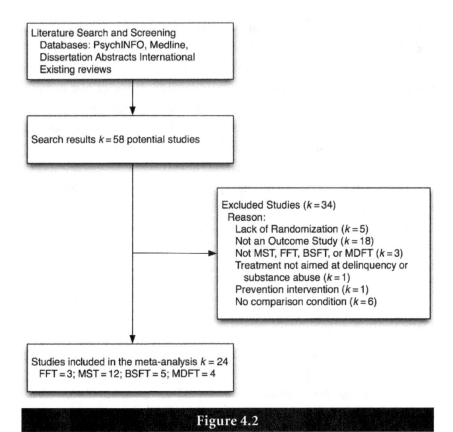

Figure 4.2

Example flow chart for a literature review. From "The Effects of Family Therapies for Adolescent Delinquency and Substance Abuse: A Meta-Analysis," by S. A. Baldwin, S. Christian, A. Berkeljon, and W. R. Shadish, 2012, *Journal of Marital and Family Therapy*, p. 286. Copyright 2012 by John Wiley & Sons. Reprinted with permission.

Method sections in papers reporting the results of an experiment or survey have the same purpose as Method sections in literature reviews; they differ only in details. When writing about your experiment, you should describe the following:

- Participants: number, characteristics, inclusion and exclusion criteria, and recruitment method
- Measures: names, type (e.g., self-report, interview, physiological), psychometric information (e.g., reliability, validity)

- Procedures: what the participants did, what the experimental manipulation was Statistical analysis: how you analyzed your data

Examples of Method sections can be found in any journal, and more details can be found in the *Publication Manual of the American Psychological Association* (APA, 2009).

Results

The Results section describes the outcome of your methods—what you actually found in your literature review or what the results of the survey were. The Results section is the heart of your paper and the reason it was written in the first place, so work hard on it. I admit that I've sometimes been a bit disappointed by my students' Results sections. They work hard on the Introduction, doing their best to justify their topic and clarify their research question. The Method section flows reasonably from their research question. But they struggle with the results. A Results section should present evidence for and against the thesis. Poorly written Results sections wander, often presenting extraneous information unrelated to the research question or not explicitly presenting important evidence about the research question itself (e.g., forgetting to report the average relapse rate in medication studies for pediatric OCD when the research question is about relapse rates).

If you are writing a literature review, the Results section should present key results from the relevant literature. Furthermore, the results should be organized to produce a narrative that addresses the research question. Think about the Results section as the narrative of a story that is organized around key plot points. What are the key plot points of your review? In my outline for the mechanisms of cognitive therapy (see Chapter 3), the three key plot points would be (a) how cognitive therapy is proposed to work, (b) methods and models for evaluating treatment mechanisms, and (c) evidence specific to the treatment mechanisms in cognitive therapy. I would draw on multiple sources for each of these topics, weaving them together to present a narrative.

A common mistake literature review writers make is organizing their Results section by source. In this type of Results section, the authors present each source one by one, and the Results section is more of a list or annotated bibliography than a coherent story. As I discussed in Chapter 3, finding quotes and summarizing each of your articles is a key part of developing your paper. It can also be a helpful first step in getting going when starting to draft your paper. However, if your final Results section consists of your summaries listed one right after another, you have a problem—you aren't making an argument or addressing the research question. The reader is forced to put the pieces of your puzzle together and figure out how each source fits with the others to answer the research question. You should be doing that for them by synthesizing the ideas from several sources.

So how do you create a narrative? I recommend four methods: analyze, evaluate, compare, and synthesize. Using these methods will help you see patterns across sources, which will help you tie them together. Your evaluations, comparisons, analysis, and synthesis, as well as the patterns you identify from these activities, can be plot points in your narrative.

First, *analyze* each of the studies, which means breaking each of them down into component parts. The parts of empirical studies include

- units: people, animals, schools, workplaces, and so forth.
- observations: outcome measures and other descriptions or characteristics of the units.
- settings: location of the study (e.g., research lab, school setting, workplace).
- procedures: treatments, experimental manipulations, survey methods.
- analyses: statistical methods, qualitative review of interviews.

Much of the material for your analysis was part of your research summaries. Once you have broken the sources down into the parts, you can group sources together. Which studies used the same outcome measures, or which studies used the same treatments? Grouping sources in this way helps you see patterns across studies.

Second, *evaluate* the sources, which involves identifying the strengths and weaknesses of each article. Your article summaries include their limitations (see Chapter 3). Do multiple studies have the same limitation (or strength)? For example, do several or all studies lack random participant assignment to conditions? Do most studies use only college students as participants? Strengths and limitations don't need to be methodological in nature. Perhaps all studies ignored important theoretical perspectives when interpreting the results.

Third, *compare* the results of the studies. Do similar studies give similar results? For example, do treatment studies that all use the same treatment manual produce similar results? Do studies that differ in methodology but are aimed at the same theoretical question produce similar results? For example, do treatment studies that use different outcome measures produce similar results? Do studies with more rigorous research designs produce different results from studies with weaker designs? For example, do treatment studies with random assignment to condition (an element of strong design) differ from treatment studies with nonrandom assignment?

Fourth, *synthesize* your studies. This is where you bring together the results of your analysis, evaluation, and comparison. Think of each study as being on a card. You are now going to sort the cards into meaningful groups. Studies may end up in just one of your groups or, more likely, will contribute to multiple categories. For example, group the studies according to the type of participants used: college students versus the general population, children versus adults, or clinical versus nonclinical populations. Other possible groupings include empirical versus theoretical articles, positive versus negative findings, methodologically weak versus strong studies, or small versus large samples. The specific groups you use will be a function of your topic area and your specific research question. The key is to synthesize or link the studies so that you can craft a narrative that addresses the research question.

The principles behind a Results section for an empirical report are identical to those for a literature review—create a narrative that addresses the research question. Because you're synthesizing analyses of original data, rather than results from published articles, the details differ. Rather than organizing studies and grouping them, you will be organizing your analyses.

Suppose you are studying memory. You ask participants to memorize a list of 20 words, but before asking them to recall the words, you expose them to other words. One group of participants reads a list of real words, and the second reads a list of nonsense words. You then ask participants to recall the words from the original list. You hypothesize that participants will recall more words when they have been exposed to nonsense words than when exposed to real words.

The Results section for this type of study will be brief and would typically follow the pattern of describe, compare, and explore. In the *describe* section, you provide descriptive statistics about the participants and their performance. You could provide demographic information about the participants (e.g., gender, age, education) and descriptive information about their performance on the memory task. In the *compare* section, you report the results of statistical comparisons between the conditions. These comparisons might include a *t* test comparing the conditions or, if you adjusted for covariates, a regression or analysis of covariance model.

Finally, your Results section would also include an *explore* section. The *explore* section could include any exploratory or sensitivity analyses you ran. For example, if you decided after collecting data that you wanted to explore whether men and women differed in their recall, you could report those analyses in this section. If two participants did so poorly at the memory task that you want to exclude them from the analyses, you could report the results excluding them here. This type of analysis is called a *sensitivity analysis* because it helps establish whether your results are sensitive to the decisions you make.

A key principle for any Results section is transparency. If you collected data on 40 participants but had to exclude two people because of errors in data collection, you should state that this is the case. If you report exploratory analyses to examine gender or age differences, you should indicate that your analyses were exploratory rather than planned from the outset of the study. Some, perhaps many, findings in psychology could be the result of exploratory analyses that capitalized on unique aspects of particular datasets (e.g., Kerr, 1998; Simmons, Nelson, & Simonsohn, 2011). Labeling results as exploratory helps remind the reader to treat those results as tentative and in need of replication. Like the Method section, the Results section should be

---

Exhibit 4.2

Adjusting the Analyze, Evaluate, Compare, and Synthesize Method for Other Types of Assignments

All types of writing need a narrative, and you can use the analyze, evaluate, compare, and synthesize approach for many kinds of writing assignments. For example:

- If you've been assigned a reaction paper, start with a thesis or main idea and then evaluate the evidence for your main idea. Is your evidence based on an anecdote, an emotional feeling, data, etc.? Do your sources of evidence agree or disagree? Can you reconcile the sources of evidence?
- If you've been assigned a book report for a nonfiction book, evaluate each of the chapters. Do the chapters support the main idea of the book? Are any chapters particularly weak? What makes them weak? What kind of evidence is reported? Do you have any ideas for how the book could be improved?

---

sufficiently transparent that someone else with your data could reproduce exactly what you report.

The analyze, evaluate, compare, and synthesize method works for assignments other than empirical papers and literature reviews. You can apply this method to other assignments, too, as shown in Exhibit 4.2.

Discussion

A Discussion section serves two purposes: (a) It summarizes and evaluates the findings, and (b) it connects the findings to the broader literature in the area. A good way to start a Discussion section is with a clear statement of what you learned from your study. For example,

> The results of this review suggest that although cognitive therapy is effective in treating depression, there is little evidence that cognitive therapy works via the hypothesized mechanisms. Mediational studies

do not support that depressive schemas are the change mechanism. Meta-analyses of treatment adherence suggest that adherence is not strongly correlated with outcome. Finally, a component study found that a full version of cognitive therapy was not more effective than stripped-down versions.

If you were studying the relationship between divorce and depression, an initial Discussion paragraph might look like the following:

> The results of this review are conflicting as to whether divorce is a cause of depression in children. Three studies supported such a relationship, two showed no relationship, and three showed that children of divorced parents were actually happier than other children.

A good Discussion section isn't limited to a summary of the results. If you limit the discussion to just a summary, it will be too similar to the Results section and will be boring. You should also evaluate the findings and weave in ideas you generated from your analysis, evaluation, and comparison of the studies or results. If you notice a pattern for particular kinds of studies or for specific outcomes in your study, comment on them. If some results seem more trustworthy than others, note this and explain your reasoning. The following extends the divorce and depression example:

> However, an interesting pattern emerges when examining the relationship between study design and study results. All the studies suggesting that divorce causes depression are large-scale epidemiological surveys with random samples. The other studies are all small surveys with samples of convenience. It may be that the results from the large random samples are more accurate.

Finally, the Discussion section should connect your findings to the broader literature. Look back at Figure 4.1; it shows that the bottom triangle starts narrow, which represents your summary and evaluation of your results. The bottom triangle ends wide, illustrating that the Discussion should comment on how your specific results fit within the literature generally. For the cognitive therapy example, you could develop the idea that researchers don't understand the mechanisms for most treatments. A topic sentence for a paragraph exploring that idea could be "Although the evidence did not suggest that cognitive therapy works via the hypothesized mechanisms, treatment mechanism research has not produced clear results for any treatment." For the depression example, you could connect your results to the broader literature on social causes of depression in children: "The correlation between divorce and depression in large studies is similar in size to those seen between socioeconomic status and depression and between other life stressors and depression."

WRITING YOUR PAPER: A WARNING

My favorite triathlon distance is what is known as the half-distance, or 70.3. In these races, you swim 1.2 miles, bike 56 miles, and then run 13.1 miles (i.e., 70.3 total miles). When I first started training for long races, I didn't have a good sense of how to train for these events. I'd jump in the pool and try to swim a mile straight, or I'd go for a long run at one (very slow) pace, hoping to run 7 or 8 or as many miles as I could go. My logic was simple: My race was long, so my preparation should mimic what I would do on race day. I got a little better with this training, but my performance in my first race was disappointing.

After the race, I did my own research about training for long endurance events, and I consulted with people who had successfully competed in these types of races. I learned that training for this kind of race requires a different kind of preparation, one that involves a mix of different kinds of training. To be sure, I still had to do a lot of swimming, biking, and running. What changed was that rather than going to the pool to swim 2,000 yards straight, I would swim sets of intervals—some sets I'd swim fast and hard, others I'd swim at race pace, and others I would swim easy so I could focus on technique. Often I would swim just as far as I used to, but I got a lot faster. Biking and running were the same—a mix of short hard efforts, some medium efforts, and then slow easy stuff. I got a lot better.

The mistake that I, like most of my colleagues and students, sometimes make is to start the writing process by opening a new document on my computer and trying to write the paper without sufficient preparation. This is just like trying to go out and get my miles in as the way to prepare for the race. I may finish the paper, just like I finished my race, but the paper, like my running form at the end of my first race, will be ugly. Sometimes just sitting down and pounding out your paper works and the material you produce is OK. Most of the time, however, the writing is crappy. Just like training for an endurance race, scientific writing requires a lot of work up front. Scientific writing reports on research, either analyzing data you've collected or reviewing the results of others. You need to know your background material, methods, and data well to produce good scientific writing. Therefore, if you have skipped Chapters 1 through 3 and the beginning of this chapter and you are just looking for advice on how to make the 10 pages go more quickly, I kindly ask you to close this chapter, turn to Chapter 1, and dive into the tough background work.

DRAFTING YOUR PAPER

If you've done what I said—read the initial chapters and completed the preparatory work—you've come a long way on your project. Now it's time to get to work on the sentences and paragraphs. I don't like to call this stage *writing*; I prefer the term *drafting*. Your task right now is to take your outline and start to flesh out some paragraphs for each part. Get the words down. Don't worry about creating a tight connection between paragraphs and making sure material flows from one idea to the next. If you have worked on your outline and mind map, and if you have organized your outline according to the Introduction, Method, Results, and Discussion structure, your paragraphs will be connected to one another and you will see the flow, which you can make even better later.

Don't worry about finding just the right word or trying to use big words. Don't even worry if you have sentence fragments or incomplete thoughts. You'll fix those later. In fiction writing, authors are often encouraged to free write, or to spend a fixed amount of time writing without any editing or stopping. The idea is to allow themselves to write without self-criticism or worries about what others will think. Many of the words they write may never make it to a final draft, but that doesn't matter—getting started is what matters. You can use the same idea—get your ideas out of your head and onto the computer. Don't worry about whether you are making grammatical errors, and don't focus on your grade. If you have done the preparatory work, then the words will come.

Sometimes my students are reluctant to try drafting in this way, but I make them do it anyway. I like to remind them of the two keys to successful drafting. First, you have to be prepared, which is what the previous chapters of this book have been all about. Writing requires content—something to write about. Preparation helps you develop that content. Imagine that I want you to write about the history of triathlon and then asked you to draft a few paragraphs of the introduction. You may be able to write a few sentences about what triathlon is, but unless you have read about it or participated in the sport, you are unlikely to have anything at all to say. Second, you actually have to *do* the drafting. You can't pretend that you are trying to write and just think through the material without putting anything down on the page.

How do you get started with drafting? The list below describes some structured activities you can use to get yourself going. I suggest that you spend about 10 minutes per activity. Writing is often slow because we try to edit and make things perfect the first time around. Limiting the time you spend drafting a particular section can help you focus on just getting the words down—you won't have the time to edit. Try it; it works.

- Pick a section of your Method section. It could be any part of the Method section, but if you are just getting started, I suggest that you describe your search methods or participants. Spend 10 minutes drafting in plain language what you did, as if you were writing a simple journal entry. "I started by searching PubMed and PsycINFO using the key words. . . ." Remember, you can make the language more professional later.
- Draft the end of the Introduction, where you describe the purpose of your paper. Spend 10 minutes drafting what you want your paper to

accomplish. I like to use plain, perhaps overly familiar language here as well: "In this paper, I will evaluate the role of stress like divorce on the development of depression. I will review the literature on. . . ."

- Choose a key quote from your background material. During your work in Chapter 3, you should have figured out a potential place to use this quote. Start by typing the quote into your document—don't just cut and paste the quote from a pdf or website; actually type it. I find that making my fingers type helps me get into the flow of writing.[2] Once the quote is in place, along with the appropriate citation (see Chapter 6), spend 10 minutes drafting the paragraph leading up to the quote and the paragraph after it. In other words, start writing what is needed to set up the quote for the preceding paragraph and what you want to say about the quote for the subsequent paragraph.

- Create a table or figure for your paper. For example, include a table summarizing the outcomes of the studies in your literature review regarding the response rate to treatment. Or include a table that reports the results of a statistical analysis, such as a correlation matrix or an analysis of variance source table. After making the table, spend 10 minutes drafting a paragraph that tells the reader what the table is about.

- Spend 10 minutes writing the first paragraph of your Discussion section. Start each sentence with the phrase "I found . . ."—for example, "I found that few studies directly compared medication treatments to psychotherapy in the treatment of pediatric OCD" or "I found that response rates to treatment were higher in adults than children." The key here is to describe the three or four main findings in your paper, and using "I found" can help you get going. Once you have the findings written out, you can go back and drop the "I found" phrases and make the paragraph flow normally.

---

[2] I got this idea from the movie *Finding Forrester*, a story about a brilliant young writer who gets mentored by a grumpy but famous writer (Connery, Tollefson, Mark, & Van Sant, 2001). I suggest that after you get your paragraphs written, you yell, "You're the man now, dawg." You must also be careful to ensure that you properly cite the quote (see Chapter 6). The character in *Finding Forrester* got in trouble because he copied some material from his mentor without explicit attribution (you'll have to watch the movie to see how that works out).

SUMMARY

Scientific writing is highly structured. This is nearly always a blessing because you don't have to spend any energy on figuring out the structure of your paper. Instead, you can focus solely on using the activities in this chapter to get your writing going. If you find yourself doubting whether you can produce the paper, try these activities to help you get started. My experience, both with my own writing and with helping students, is that if you can let go of self-criticism (or at least set it aside for a bit) and use some activities to get started, you won't have too much trouble getting each section of your paper drafted. If you still feel stuck, use your outline as a guide, and draft a paragraph for each piece of the outline. The advice and activities in this chapter will help you get started on the Introduction, Method, Results, and Discussion sections. Now you just need to fill in the rest.

5

Revising Your Paper

Now that you've drafted your paper, it's time to get to the business of revising. You have the content down, but although some of the sentences and paragraphs are in good shape, others need work. Now is the time to work on the wording of your sentences, making sure that each paragraph communicates one main idea, that all paragraphs flow logically, and that you identify and smooth over any holes in your content. I enjoy this part of writing because I find that producing content (i.e., drafting) is harder than making it clear.

In this chapter, I discuss eight rules (listed in Exhibit 5.1) for improving your writing to help guide you as you edit your papers. These rules can be broken, but generally, if you adhere to these ideas, your writing will improve.

http://dx.doi.org/10.1037/0000045-006
Writing Your Psychology Research Paper, by S. A. Baldwin

Exhibit 5.1

Eight General Rules for Improving Your Writing

1. Make sure each paragraph communicates a single idea.
2. Write in complete sentences.
3. Correct spelling errors.
4. Use the active voice.
5. Don't use sentences longer than 25 words.
6. Show, don't tell.
7. Don't write something that you don't understand or can't explain.
8. Read good writing.

MAKE SURE EACH PARAGRAPH COMMUNICATES A SINGLE IDEA

A common problem in writing is poorly developed paragraphs, with the most common problem being paragraphs that include too many ideas. For example, I recently read a paper about the treatment of substance abuse problems. The first portion of the paper gave some background about substance abuse problems, such as prevalence, theories about etiology, and prognosis. The second paragraph covered five topics: (a) diathesis–stress models, (b) genetics, (c) family environment, (d) peer group influence, and (e) stress.

The problem with five ideas in a single paragraph is twofold. First, no topic is well developed. For example, genetics is a huge topic, and most readers will need plenty of information to understand the technical details of genetic evidence (e.g., what a *heritability estimate* means). One to two sentences within a complicated paragraph do not suffice. Second, topics are not connected adequately with one another. How are family environment and genetics related? Are peers or family a major source of stress? What is the diathesis–stress model, and can it be a primary link between genetics, peers, family, and stress?

As you revise the material you have drafted, count the number of ideas in each paragraph. Compare each paragraph with the points in your outline, and ask the following questions:

- Are the ideas in the paragraphs key parts of the outline, or are they tangential? If the ideas are tangential, cut them and trim your paragraph to the key idea represented in your outline. Sometimes you add tangential material to papers because you are excited about a topic. Sometimes you add tangential material because you are worried that you will not have enough to say to fill the page requirements for assignments. Regardless, cut the tangents and focus your paragraphs.
- Have I combined several parts of my outline into a single paragraph? If you have combined several points from your outline into a single paragraph, you will likely need to split the paragraph into multiple paragraphs and better develop each idea. I have had students object to this, especially when there is a page limit on their paper: "I need to talk about genetics, peers, and stress," they may say, "but I don't have room in the paper." Page limits are not an excuse for muddled writing. You may have to cut a topic, and you may have to reorganize.

Finally, limiting paragraphs to a single idea makes them easier to read. Long, winding paragraphs, even if they are well written, can be difficult to follow. Focused paragraphs help chunk information into manageable, digestible bits. In her book *Economical Writing*, Dierdre McCloskey (2000) compared paragraphs to punctuation in sentences:

> The paragraph should be a more or less complete discussion of one topic. Paragraphing is punctuation, similar to stanzas in poetry. The stanzas can't be too long. You will want occasionally to pause for various reasons, having completed a bit of discussion, shifting the tone perhaps or simply giving the reader a break. The reader will skip around when her attention wanders, and will skip to the next paragraph. (p. 44)

Remember, writing is meant to be read, and we can help the reader out by using well-crafted paragraphs.

WRITE IN COMPLETE SENTENCES

This recommendation is simple: Write in complete sentences. If you are reading this book as part of a college class, you're probably rolling your eyes. Don't worry: I know that you know that you should write in complete sentences. I know that my students know that they should write in complete sentences. What's more, I know that I know I should write in complete sentences. Unfortunately, knowing this is not even half of the battle when it comes to errors in our writing.

We have to be vigilant in our writing and editing because incomplete sentences creep into writing more often than they should. Although you can use incomplete sentences for stylistic effect, most incomplete sentences I run into while grading class work or editing my own papers are neither stylish nor effective. They are errors. A good place to start is to turn on the grammar- and spell-checker on your computer or, if the grammar-checker is already on, to pay attention to it. Although you can't rely just on these tools, they can help you locate problems and are a simple way to make your papers a bit better.

If you choose to try to use incomplete sentences for stylish effect, I recommend McCloskey's (2000) simple advice:

> Which leads to the sentence. That is not one. Such tricks should be attempted only occasionally, and only for a reason (here: a dramatic surprise, if corny). Write mainly in complete sentences. This isn't a matter of school grammar. It's a matter of not raising expectations that you don't fulfill. As a fluent speaker of English (or at least of your dialect), you know when a sentence is a sentence by asking whether it could stand as an isolated remark. (p. 55)

CORRECT SPELLING ERRORS

It goes without saying (but I'm going to say it anyway), but good writing doesn't have spelling errors. I know that avoiding spelling errors is obvious advice, but spelling problems are common. Your spell-checker can help, and you should use it. Also, watch out for correctly spelled but incorrectly used words. Commonly misused words are *there* and *their*, *it's* and *its*, *to* and *too*, *who's* and *whose*, and *which* and *witch* (particularly a problem for fantasy writers). Your spell-checker won't catch these, so these errors will often make it through to your final draft. This means that you need to read your paper carefully. Sometimes writing feels so unpleasant that reading through what we've written is the last thing we want to do. Nevertheless, you still need to catch those errors.

USE THE ACTIVE VOICE

A hallmark of science is objectivity—scientists aren't supposed to let their personal biases and perspectives influence their studies but rather are supposed to follow wherever the results lead them. Unfortunately, scientific writing often gets bogged down with the passive voice in a misguided attempt to remove scientists themselves from appearing in papers. The logic seems reasonable: Writing should focus on the content, methods, and results, not on the people who conducted the study. This logic prompts people to use the passive voice, which doesn't actually change the substance of the paper—it just makes it less readable.

What is the passive voice? What is the active voice, which is the opposite of the passive voice? Consider two sentences:

1. Jill threw the ball.
2. The ball was thrown by Jill.

The first sentence uses the active voice, and the second uses the passive voice. Both sentences contain a subject, object, and a verb, and both connect the subject and object with a verb. Both sentences are grammatically correct.

The primary distinction between the passive and active voice is what gets assigned to be the subject of the sentence. The subject of an active voice sentence is the actor in the sentence, whereas the subject of a passive voice sentence is what is acted upon. In Sentence 1, the subject of the sentence is the actor (i.e., the person who threw the ball)—Jill—and the object of the sentence is what was acted upon (i.e., what Jill threw)—the ball. This sentence uses the active voice. It's the most direct way to explain what's happening, and therefore it's easy to follow. Sentence 2, in contrast, is in the passive voice. The subject of the sentence is the ball, and the object of the sentence is Jill. In other words, the passive voice prioritizes what is acted upon rather than the actor.

The passive voice can hide the actor altogether, and that is why it's sometimes viewed as objective, or scientific. Consider two more sentences:

1. The scientist assigned participants to the treatment conditions according to their depression level.
2. The participants were assigned to the treatment conditions according to their depression level.

Sentence 1 is in the active voice, and Sentence 2 is in the passive voice. Notice that Sentence 2 does not include an actor at all; we don't know who actually assigned participants to conditions. You can see why the passive voice could be appealing to scientists who want to appear objective, because the passive voice removes all mention of them from their writing. If the scientists drop some observations from their dataset, they can write, "Observations were removed from the dataset" rather than "We removed observations from the dataset."

Using the passive voice to appear objective has two problems. First, it is an illusion. I have not run into datasets that are self-aware and can remove observations without the help of a person. Second, the passive voice often produces clunky, hard-to-read writing. Scientific writing is hard to read as it is, given the technical nature of the material and the density of information. Don't make it worse by relying heavily on the passive voice.

To better understand why the passive voice can be a problem, think about writing you enjoy—novels, poetry, music, or movies. Is the passive voice common? No. Movies and songs don't use the passive voice because we hardly ever speak in the passive voice. The climax of the movie *A Few Good Men* (Reiner, Brown, & Scheinman, 1992) is a military courtroom scene where Lieutenant Daniel Kaffee (Tom Cruise) is questioning Colonel Jessup (Jack Nicholson) about Jessup's role in the death of a young solider. The lines in the scene are as follows (Anime Strike, 2017):

Kaffee: Colonel Jessup, did you order the Code Red?

Judge Randolph: You don't have to answer that question!

Colonel Jessup: I'll answer the question! *[to Kaffee]* You want answers?

Kaffee: I think I'm entitled to them.

Colonel Jessup: You want answers?

Kaffee: I want the truth!

Colonel Jessup: You can't handle the truth!

The scene is exciting, dramatic, and easy to follow. Now let's put that scene into the passive voice:

Kaffee: Colonel Jessup, was the Code Red ordered by you?

Judge Randolph: That question does not have to be answered by you.

Colonel Jessup: The question will be answered by me. *[to Kaffee]* Are answers wanted by you?

Kaffee: Being entitled to answers is thought of by me.

Colonel Jessup: Are answers wanted by you?

Kaffee: The truth is wanted by me!

Colonel Jessup: The truth can't be handled by you!

That sounds dumb, right? And it's much harder to follow than the active version.[1]

How do you get better at using the active voice? First, you need to be aware of the distinction between passive and active writing. You've got that covered with this section. Second, you just have to start using the active voice. Not all sentences have to be in the active voice, but many sentences will be easier to understand if they are. Sometimes you'll take a sentence in the passive voice, make it active, and find out that the active version sounds awkward or distorts clarity. Remember, however, that there is a distinction between (a) choosing to write in the passive voice because

---

[1] See Tuesday (2009) for some additional movie quotes that sound weird when translated to passive voice.

it better communicates your meaning and (b) falling into the habit of writing in the passive voice because it sounds objective and smart.

DON'T USE SENTENCES LONGER THAN 25 WORDS

Scientists present their research at conferences. A common form of presentation is to give a talk to anywhere from five to 200 scholars. As my graduate students prepare their talks, they express a common fear that goes something like this: "How am I going to speak for 20 minutes on my paper? I have only a few analyses to present. If I just stand up and present the results, I'll look dumb." Because they're afraid that they can't fill the whole 20 minutes, they start creating PowerPoint slides providing lots and lots of background information on their topic. After they practice their talk, it turns out that filling 20 minutes wasn't the problem: Keeping their talk under 40 minutes was. My students are so used to long-winded scientific talks and lectures that they have come to believe that the point of a scientific talk is to sound smart rather than to communicate ideas.

Many times we share the same fear when we write. Can I write enough? Do I have anything interesting to say? Will I sound smart? When writing is motivated by fear, we often produce wordy sentences. We write wordy sentences because it helps us fill page requirements. We write wordy sentences because they sound smart and appear to have depth. We fear short sentences because they seem too simple. In addition to causing stress, these fears lead to a problem—you guessed it, crappy writing.

Your writing isn't by definition poor because you have some sentences longer than 25 words. Plenty of good writing has more than 25 words in the sentences (see the quote that follows this paragraph). Find sentences in your paper that have more than 25 words, and evaluate whether each word has a purpose in communicating an idea. If the answer is yes, by all means, keep each word. If the answer is no, as is typical in my writing, start editing.

Zinsser (2006) recommended the following principle:

> But the secret of good writing is to strip every sentence to its cleanest components. Every word that serves no function, every word that

could be a short word, every adverb that carries the same meaning that's already in the verb, every passive construction that leaves the reader unsure of who is doing what—these are the thousand and one adulterants that weaken the strength of a sentence. (pp. 6–7)

In other words, don't forget the primary reason we write scientific papers—to communicate ideas. Therefore, the primary virtue in writing is clarity.

Here is an example, from my own writing, of a sentence that is too long and needs editing. In this paragraph, I was arguing against a common statistical practice involving a quantity called the *intraclass correlation* (ICC):

> Because proportions cannot be negative by definition, many researchers follow the practice of fixing negative ICCs to zero (cf. Maxwell & Delaney, 2004). Although interpreting the ICC as the proportion of variance attributable to therapists is conceptually compelling, it can be statistically problematic because it forces statistical dependence to be positive (Kenny, Mannetti, Pierro, Livi, & Kashy, 2002).

Both sentences need editing. In the first sentence, we could change the phrase "follow the practice of fixing" to just "fix." In the second sentence, the first clause, from "Although" to "compelling," uses a lot of words to say nothing. This is an example of a sentence that sounds smart but, when you think about it for just a bit, is empty. Thus, the edits are as follows:

> Because proportions cannot be negative by definition, many researchers ~~follow the practice of fixing~~ **fix** negative ICCs to zero (cf. Maxwell & Delaney, 2004). ~~Although interpreting the ICC as the proportion of variance attributable to therapists is conceptually compelling, it~~ **Unfortunately**, this practice can be statistically problematic because it forces statistical dependence to be positive (Kenny, Mannetti, Pierro, Livi, & Kashy, 2002).

The second sentence is far better because the edits (a) remove a clause with little meaning, (b) reduce the number of words in the sentence from 27 to 15, and (c) use one word, *unfortunately*, to communicate the evaluation I was trying to make in the original draft using 15 words.

Here's another example of a long sentence that could use some editing:

Because of the complexity of factors that impact the development and maintenance of substance use disorders, effective management for many patients requires a constellation of treatment approaches and services.

What are some of the problems with this sentence? Are there simpler ways to state the ideas? Here's one potential revision:

Because of the complexity ~~of factors that impact the development and maintenance~~ of substance use disorders, effective management for many patients requires a constellation of treatment approaches and services.

These edits shorten the sentence from 29 to 21 words. Another edit could be as follows:

Because of the complexity ~~of factors that impact the development and maintenance~~ of substance use disorders, effective ~~management for many patients~~ **treatment** requires ~~a constellation of treatment~~ **several** approaches and services.

These edits shorten the sentence to 15 words. The edited sentence provides the same information with less fluff.

Remember that the primary reason for having sentences shorter than 25 words is clarity and vigor in your writing. Below I share three suggestions for improving clarity from other books on writing. As edit your paper, try to implement these suggestions.

Eliminate Descriptive Words That Don't Add any Meaningful Description

A good place to start in strengthening your writing is eliminating adverbs that don't add meaning. *Adverbs* are words used to describe verbs, adjectives, or other adverbs. In the sentence "Jack ran quickly," "quickly" is an unnecessary adverb because its meaning is already included in the word "ran." Additionally, Silvia (2007) recommended eliminating specific descriptive words: "Delete *very, quite, basically, actually, virtually, extremely, remarkably, completely, at all,* and so forth. Basically, these quite useless words add virtually nothing at all; like weeds, they'll in fact actually smother your sentences completely" (pp. 64–65). Try removing the useless words and enjoy the strong, clear sentence that remains.

Remove Jargon and Unneeded Complex Words

Scientific ideas are complex, and it is your job as a writer to communicate those complex ideas clearly. Sometimes you can't get around using complex words because the subject matter dictates it, but often you can. Scientific fields create words or give commonly used words special meaning to communicate their ideas. These words are known as *jargon* and should be avoided if possible. More often than not, standard words do just fine. Psychologists love to use the word *affect* in place of *emotion*. I recently heard a psychologist say to one of his students, in all earnestness, that his "affect was low." As near as I could tell, all he wanted to say was that the student looked sad.

Jargon and other complex words might make writing seem smart, but they actually interfere with the primary aim to be clear. George Orwell (1946), in his essay "Politics and the English Language," suggested that writers "never use a foreign phrase, a scientific word, or a jargon word if you can think of an everyday English equivalent" (para. 16). Orwell called the use of complex words "pretentious diction" (para. 7), which conveys the sense that we sometimes use these words to communicate stature and intelligence rather than to be clear about what we mean.

Silvia (2007), in his book *How to Write a Lot*, reminded writers to pick words with an eye on clarity of expression and respect for readers:

> Writing begins and ends with words. To write well, you need to choose good words. The English language has a lot of words, and many of them are short, expressive, and familiar—write with these words. Avoid trendy phrases that sound intellectual, and never use words that make you sound like an academic psychologist. Besides improving

your writing, good words show respect for your many readers who learned English as a second, third, or fourth language. (p. 61)

Don't Use Words With More Than Four Syllables

This suggestion is directly related to the suggestion above because nearly all words with more than four syllables have simpler equivalents. Following this suggestion is pretty simple. Start by reading your paper out loud and listening for long words. Note the long words, and think of a simpler equivalent. If you get stuck, open the thesaurus on your computer and see whether there is a simpler word.

Once you start paying attention to the words you're using in your writing, you'll likely find many opportunities to use the three suggestions above. Now you must practice and practice and, after all that practice, practice some more. As I've said before, writing is a skill, and you can get better only by writing more and using the tools in this book regularly. Before you know it, you will no longer use phrases like "very small" or "virtually empty" when you draft. You'll stop looking for words that sound smart and just use the words you need instead. You get the idea—now practice.

SHOW, DON'T TELL

Evidence is the cornerstone of science. Consequently, evidence should be front and center in your writing. Rather than telling your reader about an idea, show your reader the evidence supporting the idea. Make the case for your claims, and provide citations for your claims (see Chapter 6). Table 5.1 illustrates the difference between showing and telling.

DON'T WRITE SOMETHING THAT YOU DON'T UNDERSTAND OR CAN'T EXPLAIN

Be sure you understand and can explain everything you write. Scientific theories can be detailed and nuanced—if you don't understand them, it will show. Writing something you don't understand has three major

Table 5.1

The Difference Between Showing and Telling

Telling	Showing
Depression has important societal consequences.	Depression leads to millions of dollars of lost wages and an increase in health care costs.
Side effects of psychotropic medications are a problem.	Medications can increase the risk of health problems such as diabetes.
	Severe side effects such as insomnia and sexual dysfunction often lead patients to stop taking medications.
Psychotherapy is effective.	Meta-analysis shows that more than 50% of patients respond to psychotherapy when compared with patients receiving no treatment.
The development of bipolar disorder is influenced by genetics.	Twin studies indicate that bipolar disorder has a heritability index above 70%.

problems. First, it's dishonest. We don't like it when politicians pretend to know about economic or social issues by citing studies they clearly do not understand. Your readers need to trust that you know what you mean. Second, you will struggle to defend your work. Part of writing is putting it out there for someone to read. This someone could be the professor who is going to grade it or a peer or colleague who is interested in the topic. Anyone who reads your work will have comments and criticisms, and if you don't know what you're talking about, you'll be unable to respond to feedback. Third, there's a good chance you'll be wrong. No matter how good your style is or how tight and well crafted your paragraphs are, if your content has errors, your writing will suffer.

READ GOOD WRITING

One of the best ways to improve your writing is to read good writing. You can find plenty of good writing on the web and in traditional forms. Unfortunately, you'll find bad writing as well. Your task is to find something that interests you and is well written. It doesn't matter if it's fiction or nonfiction—just find good writing. I love sports, so I like to read the blogger Bill Simmons (https://theringer.com/@BillSimmons; formerly of espn.com) as well as the Fox Sports columnist Stewart Mandel (http://www.foxsports.com/writer/stewart-mandel). Much of their writing is funny and light, and both have a clear voice and style. You won't get bogged down by verbose sentences or pretentious words as you read about professional basketball or college sports. I also enjoy a lot of the long-form writing in *The New Yorker*, especially pieces by Malcolm Gladwell and Atul Gawande.

As you expose yourself to better writing on a consistent basis, you'll start to see sections of novels that beautifully describe a scene or perfectly capture an interaction between characters. You'll also see when authors use clunky phrases or flowery language not because it's important for the scene but because it sounds important and literary (I'm looking at you, fantasy novelists). You'll appreciate when political columnists plainly explain the latest polling results or cut through the political spin when evaluating a candidate's position. You'll also start to see the positives and negatives in your own writing, which will make it easier to produce good writing.

SUMMARY

Good writing requires editing; the rules in this chapter are meant to help you focus your editing. None of these rules is sacred, and good writers sometimes violate them,[2] but following them will help your writing improve. As you write more often, you'll get a better feel for when to violate the rules, and you'll also get better at producing good writing quickly. You'll never get past the need to edit, but you will get better.

---

[2]The exception is spelling errors. Poets and fiction writers might occasionally misspell words for artistic effect, but I can't think of any reason to misspell words in scientific writing.

6

Managing Citations

All scientific writing builds on the work of others. Indeed, even the most innovative theories and research projects are influenced by preexisting work in the field. Thus, it is critical to document how previous work influenced your ideas, and failing to do so is called *plagiarism*. This chapter describes in detail what plagiarism is and helps you understand how to avoid it. It also teaches you the proper ways to cite sources in your paper.

CREATIVE WORK BUILDS ON PREVIOUS WORK

Before delving into the details of academic research paper citations, I want to illustrate how creative work builds on previous work. I draw my examples from the music and film industries.

Two popular songs, of 2013 and 2014, respectively, were "Blurred Lines" (Thicke, Williams, Harris, & Gaye, 2013) and "Uptown Funk" (Bhasker

http://dx.doi.org/10.1037/0000045-007
Writing Your Psychology Research Paper, by S. A. Baldwin

et al., 2014). Besides being popular, the songs share the distinction of having been at the center of lawsuits that claimed the creators illegally used material from other artists. Marvin Gaye's family sued Robin Thicke and Pharrell Williams, primary creators of "Blurred Lines," arguing that Thicke and Williams copied parts of Gaye's (1977) song "Got to Give It Up" without permission or contractual arrangement. A jury agreed with their claims, and Thicke and Williams were ordered to pay the Gaye family $7.4 million for Gaye's contribution to the song. Likewise, five writers of the 1979 song "Oops Upside Your Head" (Wilson, Taylor, Wilson, Simmons, & Wilson, 1979) sued the creators of "Uptown Funk" for copying portions of that song. Two writers of "Oops Upside Your Head" were awarded 15% of the royalties from "Uptown Funk," even though the portion of "Oops Upside Your Head" that was used in "Uptown Funk" was relatively small (Christman, 2015).

Although some artists disagreed with the lawsuits and the rulings because of the precedent they set, few would disagree that there is a need to appropriately credit the work of others. Given the accessibility and archiving of information online, truly new ideas are difficult to develop. Most everything one creates either has been created before or, more likely, is very similar to an existing work in the same genre. Even something as complicated as calculus was created separately by two different people— Isaac Newton and Gottfried Leibniz.

As filmmaker Kirby Ferguson (2015) documented in his video documentary *Everything Is a Remix*, beloved movies and music draw inspiration (and sometimes more than just inspiration) from existing work. For example, Ferguson showed how some of Led Zeppelin's songs took elements from other artists' work without attribution, such as Willie Dixon's (1966) "Bring It on Home," Howlin' Wolf's (1964) "Killing Floor," and Bert Jansch's (1966) "Blackwaterside." Even Zeppelin's "Stairway to Heaven" (Page & Plant, 1971) used the same opening as Spirit's "Taurus" (California, 1968; this was the subject of a later lawsuit).

Ferguson (2015) also showed how George Lucas's *Star Wars* film series drew from previous movies such as the 1930s *Flash Gordon* series and Akira Kurosawa's *Hidden Fortress* (Fujimoto & Kurosawa, 1958), *Yojimbo*

(Tanaka, Kikushima, & Kurosawa, 1961), and *Sanjuro* (Tanaka, Kikushima, & Kurosawa, 1962). These influences include editing elements (e.g., soft wipe), scenes (e.g., hiding beneath the floor), and scrolling title sequences. Although viewers seeing *Star Wars* movies for the first time may believe these were original creations of George Lucas, it is clear that Lucas relied heavily on the work of those who came before him.

If creative work generally builds on previous work, what should we do? The key ethical and legal issue in writing is plagiarism, which is misrepresenting someone else's work or ideas as your own. Many bands cover songs written by other artists. The problem with Led Zeppelin and the creators of "Blurred Lines" and "Uptown Funk" is that they did not credit the source of their inspiration (Ferguson, 2015). Likewise, all scientific writing builds on the work of others; consequently, it is critical to cite the previous theories and research that inspired and support our ideas.

AVOIDING PLAGIARISM

Plagiarism can take many forms. In the case of research papers, plagiarism can be as blatant as copying someone else's entire paper or downloading one from the Internet. It goes without saying (again, I'm still going to say it) that blatant copying is unacceptable, whether it's the entire paper, a small portion, or just a table or graphic. However, plagiarism includes even more than that; copying ideas from another's work is plagiarism. Even if all the words in your paper are your own, if you borrow ideas or concepts from other sources without proper attribution, you have plagiarized. Any time you take full credit for the thesis, evidence, or structure of your paper without acknowledging previous work constitutes plagiarism.

In addition to being unethical and dishonest, plagiarism can have serious practical consequences. Unlike the songwriters mentioned at the beginning of this chapter, you probably won't be sued for plagiarism in a student paper, but universities and colleges do have strict policies about it. Faculty who plagiarize may be sanctioned and could lose their jobs.

Students who plagiarize may receive a failing grade in a course, be disciplined by the university, or even be dismissed from the university. The American Psychological Association's (2017) *Ethical Principles of Psychologists and Code of Conduct* also prohibits plagiarism. Therefore, it is critical to learn accepted methods for citation and acknowledgment of previous work and to develop good, consistent citation habits.

WHAT TO CITE

The *Publication Manual of the American Psychological Association* (APA, 2009) provides a succinct description of what you should cite in your paper:

> Cite the work of those individuals whose ideas, theories, or research have directly influenced your work. They may provide key background information, support or dispute your thesis, or offer critical definitions and data. Citation of an article implies that you have personally read the cited work. In addition to crediting the ideas of others that you used to build your thesis, provide documentation for all facts and figures that are not common knowledge. (p. 169)

Following these general guidelines will ensure that your paper appropriately acknowledges the work of others and avoids plagiarism.

To illustrate these principles, I will use my citations for a chapter I wrote about the effects of therapists on psychotherapy outcomes for *Bergin and Garfield's Handbook of Psychotherapy and Behavior Change* (Baldwin & Imel, 2013). In this chapter, my coauthor and I reviewed how important therapists are to outcomes in psychotherapy. Careful citation was particularly important for this chapter because (a) we were not the first people to discuss therapist effects and thus needed to acknowledge the ideas of others, and (b) we reviewed most of the available research literature on this topic and thus needed to document the research that informed our chapter.

Our chapter began with a discussion of how one studies therapists' outcomes. The key thing we want to learn when studying therapist effects is how much of patients' outcome is due to the therapist. Is 5% of patients' outcomes due to which therapist the patients worked with? Is it 50%? Or as much as 80%?

Methodologists make a distinction between two kinds of studies of therapist effects. Suppose our study had three therapists: Dave, Susan, and Michelle. The first kind of study, known as a *fixed effects study*, aims to understand the differences among these three therapists and thus is limited to documenting differences among Dave, Susan, and Michelle only. The second kind of study, known as a *random effects study*, aims to use Dave, Susan, and Michelle as a proxy for all similarly trained therapists. Thus, random effects studies aim to generalize their findings beyond just Dave, Susan, and Michelle to all similarly trained therapists. It is not critical for you to fully understand the differences between fixed and random effects studies. What is critical for you to understand is that a lot of other researchers have done methodological and statistical work on fixed and random effects studies, and we drew heavily on that work when we wrote our chapter (e.g., Crits-Christoph & Mintz, 1991; Martindale, 1978; Wampold & Serlin, 2000).

As the APA *Publication Manual* points out, it was not sufficient simply to cite the articles we learned from—we also had to read them. Citing them implies that we have read and understood, to the best of our ability, the material within them. Citing work you have not read is similar to plagiarism in that you are misrepresenting yourself as having studied and understood something you have not.

Citation is not only a safeguard against plagiarism; it is also useful for providing evidence for your claims. Per APA Style, you should provide citations for material that is not well-known, even if you yourself know it well. For example, in the therapist effects chapter, we referred to averages and means. Given that the formula and concept of an average is well-known and commonplace, we did not provide a supporting reference. We also performed what is called a *meta-analysis*, which allowed us to synthesize data from many studies. Given that the methodology we used in our chapter was unique and not commonly used, we provided citations for the methods (e.g., Blitstein, Hannan, Murray, & Shadish, 2005).

EXAMPLES OF KEY CITATION TYPES

Citation in a paper involves two parts: (a) the in-text citation and (b) the bibliography or reference list citation. Examples of in-text citations are found throughout this book. In APA Style, in-text citations include the author names and publication year. Table 6.1 provides a brief overview of some of the most common in-text citation formats. You should consult the APA *Publication Manual* for a comprehensive listing of in-text citations. In many medical journals, in-text citations are represented by a number that appears in parentheses or in superscript. Once you have read a few articles with differing citation styles, you'll quickly see the similarities.

Any reference cited in your paper needs to be included in a bibliography at the end of your paper. In APA Style, references in a bibliography are listed in alphabetical order by first author. The three most common reference types are journal articles, books, and book chapters, and I provide an example and brief description of an APA-Style bibliographic reference for each next. A complete listing of reference formats can be found in the APA *Publication Manual*.

Table 6.1
Examples of APA Style In-Text Citations

Situation	In-text citation
Single author	(McCloskey, 2000)
Two authors	(Enright & Beech, 1993)
Three to five authors, first citation in the manuscript	(Shadish, Cook, & Campbell, 2002)
Three to five authors, after first citation in the manuscript	(Wampold et al., 2010)
Six or more authors, first and subsequent citations	(Foa et al., 2005)
Direct quote—add page number	(Jacobson et al., 1996, p. 295)
Author referenced in the sentence	Jacobson et al. (1996) stated . . . *or* Baldwin et al. (2012) noted . . .

Note. APA = American Psychological Association.

A bibliographic entry for a journal article looks like this (see APA, 2009, p. 198):

Baldwin, S. A., Wampold, B. E., & Imel, Z. E. (2007). Untangling the alliance–outcome correlation: Exploring the relative importance of therapist and patient variability in the alliance. *Journal of Consulting and Clinical Psychology, 75,* 842–852. http://dx.doi.org/10.1037/0022-006X.75.6.842

The order of information is as follows: authors' names (initials only for first and middle names), publication year, article title (only the first word of the sentence, the first word after a colon, or a proper noun is capitalized), journal title (capitalized and in italics), journal volume, journal issue, page numbers, and digital object identifier (DOI). The journal issue is included only if each issue of the journal begins with page 1, which is not common in psychology journals. The DOI is a unique identifier used for many digital publications, including journal articles. Not all articles you find will include a DOI, but most published in the past 10 years or so will. Figure 6.1 is an annotated screenshot from one of my articles showing where to find the relevant information.

A bibliographic entry for a book looks like this (see APA, 2009, p. 202):

Zinsser, W. (2006). *On writing well* (6th ed.). New York, NY: Harper Perennial.

Figure 6.1

Example of where to find bibliographic information on an article.

The order of information is as follows: authors, publication year, title (in italics; only the first word of the sentence, the first word after a colon, or a proper noun is capitalized), edition number (if it is the second or a subsequent edition), place of publication, and publisher.

Finally, a bibliographic entry for a book chapter looks like this (see APA, 2009, p. 202):

Baldwin, S. A., & Imel, Z. E. (2013). Therapist effects: Findings and methods. In M. J. Lambert (Ed.), *Bergin and Garfield's handbook of psychotherapy and behavior change* (6th ed., pp. 258–297). New York, NY: Wiley.

The order of information is as follows: authors, year of publication, title of chapter, book editor (with initials preceding the last name), book title, edition number (for 2nd edition and greater), page numbers, place of publication, and publisher.

SOFTWARE OPTIONS FOR MANAGING CITATIONS

Depending on the length and style of your paper, managing references and citations can be difficult. When the number of references gets large, it is easy to forget to place a reference in the bibliography or a citation in the body of the text. Fortunately, several programs exist that help manage citation information, format in-text citations, and produce accurate bibliographies. The three most common programs used in my courses and among my colleagues are Zotero, EndNote, and Mendeley. APA Style Central, a new tool for learning about, teaching, writing, and publishing in APA Style, has software programs that manage citations.

The feature sets of these three programs are roughly the same, and thus they will likely be equally useful. I focus on Zotero here because it is fully open source and free (Mendeley is also free, but I have not used it as extensively as Zotero). Zotero can be used either as a standalone application or as an extension to the Firefox web browser (http://www.firefox.com). The Zotero features I use most are (a) collecting citation information, (b) producing in-text citations, and (c) formatting bibliographies.

Typing and checking citation information is tedious and error prone. Zotero aims to make the process simpler. Suppose you're writing a paper on the psychological treatment of chronic fatigue syndrome. Your search of relevant articles leads you to a cost-effectiveness study of a four-condition randomized trial of treatments for chronic fatigue (McCrone et al., 2012), which is in the journal *PLOS ONE*.[1] You navigate to the web page to download the file. Without a program like Zotero, you would need to download the article and manually type the bibliographic information into your paper. However, Zotero includes a tool that automatically extracts bibliographic information from web pages such as journal article pages, scientific databases (e.g., PsycINFO, PubMed), and booksellers (e.g., Amazon).

As you populate your Zotero database with bibliographic information, you can use that information to create in-text citations with tools that work in Microsoft Word and LibreOffice. For example, after installing the plug-in for Word, you can cite one or more references directly in your text (all references in this book were initially formatted with Zotero). You can select the citation style you would like to use, such as APA Style. If you need to switch the citation style for some reason, Zotero automatically reformats your citations for you. You can even alter the look of the in-text citation style if you need to add something to a citation (such as "e.g.," "i.e.," or a page number) or if you want to remove the author name because it is included in the text.

After you have added citations to your manuscript, you can use Zotero to create a reference list. You select the location within your manuscript where you want the reference list to appear, and Zotero adds the full bibliographic information in the style you requested. Zotero's APA Style templates are excellent but not foolproof. Consequently, you should review your citations and reference list for errors. For example, Zotero occasionally capitalizes all words in a journal article title because Zotero imported the title that way. You must go through your database and correct any errors and then have Zotero update your reference list in your paper. Regardless of the specific problem, in the end, it's your responsibility to produce an accurate document.

---

[1] I did not choose this example at random. This randomized trial, known as the PACE trial, has been heavily criticized and is the source of controversy (Coyne, 2015).

SUMMARY

Appropriate citation is critical to scientific writing. It helps the reader (and the author) document where the ideas and data came from. Proper citation also helps you build your readers' trust—trust that you have studied the literature and understand its complexities. This chapter has provided some basic rules for when you should cite a source and how you should cite the source in your writing. With some practice, citing will become second nature.

THREE

STAYING ON TASK

7

Dealing With Procrastination

Writing a paper is a lot of work. Although I've written a book on writing, I'm fully aware that it can be difficult, tedious, and downright boring. This makes the prospect of writing a paper akin to that of doing laundry or math homework. And as with your math homework or the laundry, you may even feel like putting the writing assignment off and doing something else, anything else. In fact, laundry may seem more appealing than writing, and you'll find yourself folding underwear rather than reading articles or outlining. Sure, doing laundry is important, but if you spend the days or weeks after receiving a writing assignment watching Netflix and folding undies instead of working on your paper, you're going to be in trouble. When you have to stay up all night writing your paper in order to turn it in on time, you might begin to regret not having started on it sooner. That regret might sting a bit more when you get your grade. The long-term consequences of procrastination can be a problem (e.g., falling behind,

http://dx.doi.org/10.1037/0000045-008
Writing Your Psychology Research Paper, by S. A. Baldwin

getting poor grades, not learning the material) and typically outweigh the short-term benefits (e.g., relief from boredom, reduction in anxiety).

In my courses, the biggest difference between papers that receive As and Bs and those that get Cs, Ds, or Fs is the amount of work students put into the paper well before it's due. Those who are able to put in regular, consistent effort on their papers tend to produce far better writing than those who scramble to throw together a paper at the last minute. Regular, consistent effort means that students can attend to the writing process I've outlined in this book. Such students allow sufficient time to perform the necessary background research, to develop the ideas in their paper via brainstorming and outlining, and to draft and rewrite. They catch more spelling errors. All parts of the papers are better. More importantly, those who put in the consistent effort learn more. Learning lasts longer when it is distributed over time (Cepeda, Pashler, Vul, Wixted, & Rohrer, 2006). This means that just as you forget the information you "learn" cramming for exams as soon as the exam is over, whipping together a paper tends to produce limited learning.

Sometimes instructors have intermediate deadlines for papers—the topic is due in the first few weeks of class, the Introduction a few weeks later, the Method section a few weeks after that, and so on. This structure can ensure that students are not scrambling to produce a complete paper all at the end of the course. Unfortunately, some students turn these intermediate deadlines into five or six chances to procrastinate rather than a structure to facilitate consistent, regular effort.

Like many problems in life, procrastination can feel automatic and out of our control. You didn't set out to skip working on the paper Friday afternoon to hang out at the park, but it had been a long week, it was spring, and the weather was good. You probably set aside a couple of hours Saturday morning to work on your paper, but your neighbor invited you to breakfast, then you ran to the grocery store, and then you got caught up on your Twitter feed. Suddenly it's 5 p.m., and you haven't gotten anything done. But who wants to do homework on Saturday night? And so it goes.

As with any challenging behavior, the first key to making a change is to become aware of when you are procrastinating so you can more easily make a different choice. When trying to make a change, it can also be useful to have an understanding of why you procrastinate. Psychologists have studied procrastination and have theories about why people procrastinate. This chapter will help you notice when you're procrastinating and explain the likely reasons why you're doing it, touching on a theory of procrastination that has received empirical support. I also discuss some suggestions for becoming more consistent in your writing and studying generally.

TEMPORAL MOTIVATION THEORY OF PROCRASTINATION

Throughout a day, you have many choices about how to spend your time. How much time do you want to spend sleeping, eating, working, studying, exercising, relaxing, or socializing? Temporal motivation theory (TMT) suggests that how you allocate time to each of these activities is a function of the utility of the activity (Steel, 2007). *Utility* refers to how desirable or attractive a particular activity is. In essence, if you're hungry, eating has high utility, meaning you are very motivated to eat and probably won't procrastinate doing so. If you have an exam tomorrow, studying has high utility. You might choose to stay up late to study, even though you're tired, if you value preparing for an exam more than getting a full night's sleep.

According to TMT, utility is a function of four factors: (a) the expectancy of the activity, (b) the value of the activity, (c) the delay of the rewards of the activity, and (d) your sensitivity to delayed rewards (Steel, 2007, p. 71). *Expectancy* refers to your beliefs about what the result of the activity will be. When you expect that you can successfully complete a task, the utility of the task goes up. For example, if you believe that you can make a tasty grilled cheese sandwich when you're hungry, cooking your own lunch has high utility. However, if you do not believe that you can write a 10-page paper, working on your paper will have low utility. The *value* of an activity is what it sounds like—if you value feeling full, eating will have high utility. Likewise, if you value getting a good grade or learning something, working on your paper will have high utility.

The greater the *delay of the rewards* of an activity, the lower the utility of that activity. Working on a paper that is due in 3 months does not produce immediate rewards, and thus the utility of working on the paper is low. However, if you're anxious about the paper and want to feel like you're making progress, working on the paper may reduce your anxiety today, which would increase the utility of working on the paper. Finally, if your sensitivity to delayed rewards is particularly low, activities will tend to have lower utility for you than for people who can patiently wait for the delayed rewards. That is, having an impulsive personality will magnify any delays in reward, meaning that the utility of activities will be low (Steel, 2007).

Steel (2007) illustrated how these variables work together:

> [Thomas Delay] is a college student who has been assigned an essay on September 15th, the start of a semester, due on December 15th, when the course ends. To simplify matters, Tom has two choices over the course of semester: studying or socializing. Tom likes to social- ize, but he likes to get good grades even more. However, because the positive component of socializing is perpetually in the present, it maintains a uniformly high utility evaluation. The reward of writing is initially temporally distant, diminishing its utility. Only toward the deadline do the effects of discounting decrease, and writing becomes increasingly likely. (p. 71)

In other words, when the situation is reduced to two choices—socializing and studying—Tom will choose socializing until the rewards (or fear of negative consequences) become sufficiently close in time that Tom begins to prioritize studying.

To add some complexity to this situation, suppose that Tom doesn't believe he is a good writer and finds sitting down to work on the paper aversive because he considers writing boring and tedious. Also, writing creates anxiety that he will not receive a good grade on his paper, which means he won't get a good grade in the class, which in turn will make it difficult for Tom to get into the law school he wants. If he's anxious about his performance, wouldn't it make sense for him to hunker down in the library and get writing? That way, he could devote the time he needs to overcome his fears about not being a good writer and ensure that he writes a good paper. But he decides to socialize Friday afternoon instead of working on his paper. And then he finds something else to do on Saturday rather than work on his paper. Why would he do that?

An answer to this question lies in the utility of the options. Working on the paper brings the negative experiences of boredom, tedium, and anxiety. Spending time with friends, especially since he promised himself that he'll work on the paper later, removes the boredom, tedium, and anxiety and might even introduce some fun. In short, spending time with friends will feel better than writing.

Avoidance of negative experiences is a powerful motivator in every person's life (Hayes & Smith, 2005). It might seem rational for Tom to just jump into his writing assignment, but Tom, like all of us, isn't always motivated by what is rational—Tom is affected by what is pleasant or unpleasant (Hayes & Smith, 2005). Writing produces, at least initially, negative experiences, and thus its utility is low. Socializing produces, at least initially, positive experiences, and thus its utility is high. Therefore, Tom, the poor guy, will procrastinate.

WHAT TO DO ABOUT PROCRASTINATION

TMT suggests that four things can be addressed to help deal with procrastination: expectancy, value, delay of rewards, and sensitivity to delayed rewards. I'm going to ignore your sensitivity to delayed rewards. If your impulsivity is sufficiently problematic as to rise to the level of meeting criteria for attention-deficit/hyperactivity disorder, you may need medication or a behavioral intervention from a therapist. However, expectancy, value, and delay of rewards are all things that you can address.

Let's start with value. The first thing to do is to have an honest conversation with yourself about how much you care about the assignment and why you care about it. Do you care primarily because this a required class and you just want to get through it? Do you have a genuine interest in the topic and want to learn more? Does this assignment fit within your priorities? Are there other papers due this semester or other demanding classes? Are there other demands on your time, like work, relationships, or extracurricular activities? The key is to be honest with yourself. Doing so will help you understand the utility of the writing assignment for your current circumstances.

As a clinical psychologist, I see people who have lots of different problems and who vary in how much they want to change. I once saw a man who would burn himself when he got depressed or scared. The treatment team and I suggested a number of well-established, empirically supported interventions, but we simply could not get him to commit to trying them. When I confronted him about this, he told me that he didn't care about the burning, and the primary reason he was seeking therapy was to appease his parents—they wouldn't help him financially if he didn't seek treatment.

My primary intervention at this point was to see whether he could find a part of himself that cared about getting better, the part of himself that didn't want to burn himself when he was depressed. If you simply do not care at all about the writing assignment or becoming a better writer, no intervention about time scheduling or breaking up the assignment into manageable pieces is going to help—the assignment will always have low utility. If there is a part of you that cares, that wants to make the most of this assignment, then you want to figure out how to emphasize that part of you in order to increase the utility of the assignment.

Assuming that you care about the assignment,[1] which I suspect most readers of this book do, you can start working on your expectancy and the delay of rewards and punishments. In the case of expectancy, increasing your self-efficacy regarding your ability to write comes best from regular, deliberate practice (Ericsson, Krampe, & Tesch-Römer, 1993). I argued in the introduction to this chapter that writing is a skill. As with any skill, the best way to learn how write better is to practice and to practice often. My son wanted to learn to play the guitar, so he bought a cheap electric guitar,

---

[1] I want to emphasize that not caring is perfectly fine. I hope you care about most of your assignments, though, because college will be a major chore if you don't. However, there are plenty of things I do simply out of compliance. In those cases, I just have to grit my teeth, get through them, and move on to the things I truly care about.

a small amp, and the video game Rocksmith (2012). Rocksmith lets you connect your electric guitar to a video game console and learn to play songs via various games. Rocksmith emphasizes that you will improve by practicing for short periods of time (less than an hour a day) rather than binge practicing multiple hours once or twice a week. My son took that to heart and has practiced most days for 20 to 30 minutes, usually right after dinner and homework, and in 3 months is already playing multiple songs. It is quite impressive, and it has improved his self-efficacy regarding the guitar. For my son, the guitar is no longer a mysterious instrument that requires his hands to contort and move so quickly that it looks impossible. Playing the guitar is still challenging, but now he believes he is capable of learning what he needs to, and that makes playing the guitar more fun.[2]

For most people, writing will never be as fun as playing an instrument or competing in sports. However, you get better at writing by writing. Books like this may guide you through the process of becoming a better writer, but you can't do it just by reading the book, just as you can't expect to read a book about the guitar and be able to play "Stairway to Heaven." I wish that just reading this book would make you feel supremely confident and enthusiastic about writing, but that's probably not going to happen. What this book can do is help you get started on getting this paper done. After you've done this two, three, or four times, writing a paper may continue to be difficult, but you'll know you are capable of doing it, and doing it well.

Start by committing to regular work on your writing project (Silvia, 2007). Let's say you have 1 month to complete your paper. Follow the recipe my son used for learning the guitar. For the first week, spend 30 minutes a day over 5 days working on your paper. It doesn't have to be at the same time each day, but I do find that practicing at the same time each day makes it easier to be consistent. At the end of the 5 days, you'll have worked 2.5 hours on your paper. You can get a lot done in 2.5 hours. But because you're working only 30 minutes a day, the boredom and tedium barely have time to set in.

---

[2]Check out "Rocksmith: Audrey's Success Story" (2016) for another cool story of regular practice using Rocksmith. The girl in this video was not born to play the guitar but got better by practicing.

The key concept for this strategy is consistency. Find a time, make it sacred, and work on your project. Do this even if you don't feel like it. Few people feel like writing papers. The people who get the most out of writing and who feel successful at writing are those who do it regularly and consistently. As Silvia (2007) noted,

> Instead of *finding* time to write, *allot* time to write. . . . Each person will have a different set of good times for writing, given his or her other commitments. *The secret is the regularity, not the number of days or number of hours.* (pp. 12–13, emphasis in original)

To make the most of your 30 minutes, set a goal for what you'll do during your writing time (cf. Silvia, 2007). The plan of simply going into the 30 minutes to "work on my project" will likely be too diffuse and vague to be effective. If you follow the instructions in this book, you can set goals based on the specific steps in the writing process. Examples of goals drawn from this book are as follows:

- Spend 25 minutes brainstorming and 5 minutes selecting the topic (Chapter 1).
- Reread a chapter of your textbook looking for possible topics (Chapter 1).
- Develop and test search terms for your topic (Chapter 2).
- Get search training from a librarian (Chapter 2).
- Read and take notes on two articles (Chapter 3).
- Draft your outline or create a mind map (Chapter 3).
- Draft three or four versions of a thesis statement (Chapter 3).
- Revise your outline to fit the required structure of your paper (Chapter 4).
- Draft sections of your paper (e.g., Introduction, Method; Chapter 4).
- Edit the paragraphs in your paper so that each communicates a single idea (Chapter 5).
- Reduce wordiness in your writing (Chapter 5).

Obviously, some of these goals will be more appropriate later on in the writing process. The key is to make sure you have a focus for your writing. It may seem like too much to write a 10-page paper. However, using 30 minutes to develop some search terms is a pretty manageable task. This strategy will increase your self-efficacy and make it easier for you to jump in and get some work done.

Once you've completed a week's worth of work, take a look at what you've accomplished. Are you ready to outline now? Are you ready to start drafting? Plan out the next week and commit to 5 more days of work. Set additional goals or repeat any parts of the project that still need work. You may need to increase the total time you work each day, or at least some of the days, each week. My experience in my own work and talking with students is that 30 to 60 minutes is a good time frame. Up to 1 hour isn't too intimidating but also provides enough time to get things done. If your assignment has intermediate deadlines (e.g., submit an outline), then prioritize that deadline. Repeat this process until you have completed your project.

Reducing the delay of rewards is conceptually simple but can be challenging to implement. It is easy to reduce the delay of rewards if your professor requires that the paper be completed in stages, with several intermediate deadlines. Failing to meet those deadlines means a poorer grade. Successfully meeting the deadlines not only means a better grade but also will increase your confidence in the writing process because you will see the paper coming together.

If your professor does not include intermediate deadlines, then you should create your own as a means to discourage procrastination. Sticking to your self-imposed deadlines is the challenging part—it's pretty easy to let yourself off the hook if you fail to meet such a deadline. I suggest that you have an honest conversation with yourself—it can even be out loud; I won't judge. Commit to yourself about how you will handle the deadlines, bearing in mind that skirting the deadlines will only cause you grief later on.

I find it easiest to give myself small rewards for completing tasks and maybe a large reward for completing a week's worth of work or at the end of a project. On a small level, examples of rewards I've used are

- buying myself a soda after working on a difficult project for the day's scheduled time,
- taking a break after the day's scheduled time by reading with my daughter,
- going on a short walk,
- talking with a friend,

- watching 10 to 15 minutes of a good show, and
- spending a little extra time at lunch chatting with a friend.

Examples of larger rewards I've used include

- going out for dinner or ice cream,
- taking a day off (at the end of a major writing project, such as a grant or book),
- buying myself a new book, and
- buying tickets to a concert.

The specifics of the rewards are not critical. The key thing for short-term rewards is that they be immediate and consistent. Regardless of the size of the reward, it is critical it be available only if you have completed the work. You don't want to be reinforcing ineffective behavior like procrastination.

You may notice that most of the rewards I listed are arbitrary. Getting a soda is not a natural consequence of completed scheduled work. I find that the sense of accomplishment I feel after completing work is far more reinforcing than sodas or walks. Likewise, the peace of mind I feel when I make consistent progress toward a large goal and the satisfaction I feel from having learned something are both reinforcing. The only way you will know what works for you is to give it a try. Once you reduce the time between your behavior and the rewards, I think you'll see that it isn't as hard to resist procrastination as you may think.

SUMMARY

I don't know anyone who doesn't procrastinate. Unfortunately, some people procrastinate to the point that it is dysfunctional—they struggle to meet their goals (e.g., they consistently receive poor grades in their courses, which delays or prevents graduation). Dealing with procrastination is straightforward—start working, but work in small chunks and make sure the rewards are not too distant. This strategy will reduce your fears and unease about your paper. The paper may still be tough, but it will be more manageable.

Conclusion

The late William Zinsser (2006), a prominent teacher of writing non-fiction, described writing as a "craft." He resisted the romantic notion of writing, in which inspiration and inborn gifts determine the quality of writing. Rather, he conceived of writing as a skill that requires practice, patience, and work. Skills do not spring fully formed from within us; we start at a basic level and build our way up, sometimes to excellence and sometimes to mediocrity.

I reflected on this process recently while watching wood flooring being installed in my home. In my first home, my wife and I had ripped out the carpet and linoleum in our kitchen and living room and installed wood flooring. This was the first time we had installed flooring, and we were slow. We learned how to install the flooring in a manner of minutes, but actually doing it took much longer. We hadn't anticipated the challenge of dealing with irregular cabinets, fine cuts with a jigsaw, and the finish work required where the flooring met the stairs. Further, we made lots of mistakes that required extra time to fix. It took us nearly a week to install 700 square feet of this material.

About 7 years later, our dishwasher leaked and ruined our floor. We reluctantly bought new flooring and set out to install our second floor.

http://dx.doi.org/10.1037/0000045-009
Writing Your Psychology Research Paper, by S. A. Baldwin

This time it went much better. It took us only a couple of days—we were more confident with our measurements and cuts and more skilled using the tools.

Recently, we bought a new house and had some wood flooring installed. We watched the installer work. He installed nearly double the amount we'd done the first time in less than a day. He moved quickly, made cuts with confidence, and repaired mistakes immediately. He had mastered his craft.

Was this man born to install wood flooring? It seems silly even to ask. He was good at installing floors because he installed floors every day. He was confident with his tools and his measurements and wasn't bothered by cabinets and closets that required adjustments and unique cuts. He developed his skill through practice, learning how to plan and prepare for the installation, getting feedback from supervisors, and making mistakes and fixing them. Writing is the same.

Some still hold a romantic vision of writing and of authors as poets, storytellers, comedians, or hard-hitting investigative journalists. What's more, they think writing is a calling and that authors are born, not made, and inspired daily with good ideas: not exactly the vision most students have of themselves when assigned a research paper, nor is it the vision of most teachers and scientists I know. Writing is hard; coming up with good ideas is hard; staring at a blank document on the computer is hard. I've had to work at getting better at writing, and some days (maybe most) I wish writing was easier.

As a college professor, I write—a lot. In some ways, a college professor is a writer first and foremost. We write research papers, books, lecture notes, exams, memos, and letters. I spend 6 to 8 hours a week in the classroom, and most of the rest of my time is spent writing in some form. Given my reflections in this book, you might wonder whether I enjoy my job or get satisfaction from writing. I do. However, my satisfaction comes from tackling something challenging and producing something concrete that is useful to my students and colleagues. My hope is that the suggestions in this book will make the writing process a little more pleasant than it otherwise would have been so that your writing is fulfilling and helps you learn about a topic you care about.

References

Abramowitz, J. S., & Jacoby, R. J. (2014). *Obsessive–compulsive disorder in adults.* Boston, MA: Hogrefe.

American Psychiatric Association. (2013). *Diagnostic and statistical manual of mental disorders* (5th ed.). Arlington, VA: American Psychiatric Publishing.

American Psychological Association. (2009). *Publication manual of the American Psychological Association* (6th ed.). Washington, DC: Author.

American Psychological Association. (2017). *Ethical principles of psychologists and code of conduct* (2002, Amended June 1, 2010 and January 1, 2017). Retrieved from http://www.apa.org/ethics/code/index.aspx

Anime Strike. (2017). *A Few Good Men: Quotes.* Retrieved from http://www.imdb.com/title/tt0104257/quotes

Antony, M., Downie, F., & Swinson, R. (1998). Diagnostic issues and epidemiology in obsessive–compulsive disorder. In R. Swinson, M. Antony, S. Rachman, & M. Richter (Eds.), *Obsessive–compulsive disorder: Theory, research, and treatments* (pp. 3–32). New York, NY: Guilford Press.

Author retracts study of changing minds on same-sex marriage after colleague admits data were faked. (2015, May 28). Retrieved from http://retractionwatch.com/2015/05/20/author-retracts-study-of-changing-minds-on-same-sex-marriage-after-colleague-admits-data-were-faked/

Baldwin, S. A., Christian, S., Berkeljon, A., & Shadish, W. R. (2012). The effects of family therapies for adolescent delinquency and substance abuse: A meta-analysis. *Journal of Marital and Family Therapy, 38*, 281–304. http://dx.doi.org/10.1111/j.1752-0606.2011.00248.x

Baldwin, S. A., & Imel, Z. E. (2013). Therapist effects: Findings and methods. In M. J. Lambert (Ed.), *Bergin and Garfield's handbook of psychotherapy and behavior change* (6th ed., pp. 258–297). New York, NY: Wiley.

Baldwin, S. A., Wampold, B. E., & Imel, Z. E. (2007). Untangling the alliance–outcome correlation: Exploring the relative importance of therapist and patient variability in the alliance. *Journal of Consulting and Clinical Psychology, 75,* 842–852. http://dx.doi.org/10.1037/0022-006X.75.6.842

Beck, A. T., Rush, A. J., Shaw, B. E., & Emery, G. (1979). *Cognitive therapy of depression.* New York, NY: Guilford Press.

Bender, L. (Producer), & Van Sant, G. (Director). (1997). *Good Will Hunting* [Motion picture]. United States: Miramax Films.

Bhasker, J., Lawrence, P., Mars, B., Ronson, M., Williams, N., . . . Taylor, R. (2014). Uptown funk [Recorded by M. Ronson & B. Mars]. On *Uptown special* [CD]. New York, NY: RCA.

Blitstein, J. L., Hannan, P. J., Murray, D. M., & Shadish, W. R. (2005). Increasing the degrees of freedom in existing group randomized trials: The df* approach. *Evaluation Review, 29,* 241–267. http://dx.doi.org/10.1177/0193841X04273257

Bohannon, J. (2015, May 28). Science retracts gay marriage paper without agreement of lead author LaCour. Retrieved from http://www.sciencemag.org/news/2015/05/science-retracts-gay-marriage-paper-without-agreement-lead-author-lacour

Breckman, A., & Hoberman, D. (Executive producers). (2002–2009). *Monk.* New York, NY: USA Network.

Butcher, J. N., Mineka, S., & Hooley, J. M. (2010). *Abnormal psychology* (14th ed.). Boston, MA: Pearson.

California, R. (1968). Taurus [Recorded by Spirit]. On *Spirit* [Vinyl]. New York, NY: Epic Records.

Cepeda, N. J., Pashler, H., Vul, E., Wixted, J. T., & Rohrer, D. (2006). Distributed practice in verbal recall tasks: A review and quantitative synthesis. *Psychological Bulletin, 132,* 354–380. http://dx.doi.org/10.1037/0033-2909.132.3.354

Christman, E. (2015, May 1). "Uptown Funk!" gains more writers after Gap Band's legal claim. *Billboard.* Retrieved from http://www.billboard.com/biz/articles/6553523/uptown-funk-gains-five-co-writers

Connery, S., Tollefson, R., Mark, L. (Producers), & Van Sant, G. (Director). (2000). *Finding Forrester* [Motion picture]. United States: Columbia Pictures.

Coy, P. (2013, April 18). FAQ: Reinhart, Rogoff, and the Excel error that changed history. *Bloomberg.* Retrieved from http://www.bloomberg.com/bw/articles/2013-04-18/faq-reinhart-rogoff-and-the-excel-error-that-changed-history

Coyne, J. C. (2015, December 13). Why I don't know how PLOS will respond to authors' refusal to release data [Web log post]. Retrieved from http://linkis.com/wordpress.com/8gxwn

Creed, T. A., & Kendall, P. C. (2005). Therapist alliance-building behavior within a cognitive–behavioral treatment for anxiety in youth. *Journal of Consulting and Clinical Psychology, 73,* 498–505. http://dx.doi.org/10.1037/0022-006X.73.3.498

Crits-Christoph, P., & Mintz, J. (1991). Implications of therapist effects for the design and analysis of comparative studies of psychotherapies. *Journal of Consulting and Clinical Psychology, 59,* 20–26. http://dx.doi.org/10.1037/0022-006X.59.1.20

Dixon, W. (1966). Bring it on home [Vinyl]. Chicago, IL: Checker.

Dobson, K. S. (1989). A meta-analysis of the efficacy of cognitive therapy for depression. *Journal of Consulting and Clinical Psychology, 57,* 414–419.

Dougherty, D. D., Rauch, S. L., & Jenike, M. A. (2007). Pharmacological treatments for obsessive–compulsive disorder. In P. E. Nathan & J. M. Gorman (Eds.), *A guide to treatments that work* (2nd ed., pp. 447–474). New York, NY: Oxford University Press.

EndNote [Computer software]. Philadelphia, PA: Clarivate Analytics. Retrieved from http://endnote.com

Enright, S. J., & Beech, A. R. (1993). Reduced cognitive inhibition in obsessive–compulsive disorder. *British Journal of Clinical Psychology, 32,* 67–74. http://dx.doi.org/10.1111/j.2044-8260.1993.tb01028.x

Ericsson, K. A., Krampe, R. T., & Tesch-Römer, C. (1993). The role of deliberate practice in the acquisition of expert performance. *Psychological Review, 100,* 363–406. http://dx.doi.org/10.1037/0033-295X.100.3.363

Ferguson, K. (Director). (2015). *Everything is a remix remastered* [Video documentary]. Retrieved from https://vimeo.com/139094998

Foa, E. B., Liebowitz, M. R., Kozak, M. J., Davies, S., Campeas, R., Franklin, M. E., . . . Tu, X. (2005). Randomized, placebo-controlled trial of exposure and ritual prevention, clomipramine, and their combination in the treatment of obsessive–compulsive disorder. *The American Journal of Psychiatry, 162,* 151–161. http://dx.doi.org/10.1176/appi.ajp.162.1.151

Food Babe. (2012). Why it's time to throw out your microwave [Web log post]. Retrieved from https://archive.is/SmN0x#selection-685.0-685.41

Food Babe. (2017). Break free from the hidden toxins in your food [Web log post]. Retrieved from http://foodbabe.com/tag/break-free-from-the-hidden-toxins-in-your-food/

Franklin, M. E., & Foa, E. (2007). Cognitive behavioral treatment of obsessive–compulsive disorder. In P. E. Nathan & J. M. Gorman (Eds.), *A guide to treatments that work* (3rd ed., pp. 431–446). New York, NY: Oxford University Press.

Franklin, M. E., & Foa, E. (2008). Obsessive–compulsive disorder. In D. H. Barlow (Ed.), *Clinical handbook of psychological disorders: A step-by-step treatment manual* (4th ed., pp. 164–215). New York, NY: Guilford Press.

Fujimoto, S., Kurosawa, A. (Producers), & Kurosawa, A. (Director). (1958). *The hidden fortress* [Motion picture]. Japan: Toho.

Gaye, M. (1977). Got to give it up [Vinyl]. Detroit, MI: Tamla.

Godfrey, W., Bowen, M. (Producer), & Boone, J. (Director). (2014). *The fault in our stars* [Motion picture]. United States: 20th Century Fox.

Grayson, J. (2014). *Freedom from obsessive compulsive disorder.* New York, NY: Penguin.

Green, J. (2012). *The fault in our stars.* New York, NY: Dutton Books.

Harold B. Lee Library. (2017). Keywords [Tutorial]. Provo, UT: Brigham Young University. Retrieved from http://net.lib.byu.edu/tutorial/keywords/

Hayes, S. C., & Smith, S. (2005). *Get out of your mind and into your life: The new acceptance and commitment therapy.* Oakland, CA: New Harbinger.

Hershfield, J., & Corboy, T. (2013). *The mindfulness workbook for OCD: A guide to overcoming obsessions and compulsions using mindfulness and cognitive behavioral therapy.* Oakland, CA: New Harbinger.

Hollon, S. D., DeRubeis, R. J., & Evans, M. D. (1987). Causal mediation of change in treatment for depression: Discriminating between nonspecificity and noncausality. *Psychological Bulletin, 102,* 139–149. http://dx.doi.org/10.1037/0033-2909.102.1.139

Hollon, S. D., DeRubeis, R. J., Shelton, R. C., Amsterdam, J. D., Salomon, R. M., O'Reardon, J. P., . . . Gallop, R. (2005). Prevention of relapse following cognitive therapy vs medications in moderate to severe depression. *Archives of General Psychiatry, 62,* 417–422. http://dx.doi.org/10.1001/archpsyc.62.4.417

Howlin' Wolf. (1964). Killing floor [Vinyl]. Chicago, IL: Chess.

Influential Reinhart–Rogoff economics paper suffers spreadsheet error. (2013, April 18). Retrieved from http://retractionwatch.com/2013/04/18/influential-reinhart-rogoff-economics-paper-suffers-database-error/

Jacobson, N. S., Dobson, K. S., Truax, P. A., Addis, M. E., Koerner, K., Gollan, J. K., . . . Prince, S. E. (1996). A component analysis of cognitive–behavioral treatment for depression. *Journal of Consulting and Clinical Psychology, 64,* 295–304. http://dx.doi.org/10.1037/0022-006X.64.2.295

Jansch, B. (1966). Blackwaterside. On *Jack Orion* [Vinyl]. London, England: Transatlantic.

Kenny, D. A., Mannetti, L., Pierro, A., Livi, S., & Kashy, D. A. (2002). The statistical analysis of data from small groups. *Journal of Personality and Social Psychology, 83,* 126–137.

Kerr, N. L. (1998). HARKing: Hypothesizing after the results are known. *Personality and Social Psychology Review, 2,* 196–217.

Krugman, P. (2013, April 18). The Excel depression. *The New York Times.* Retrieved from http://www.nytimes.com/2013/04/19/opinion/krugman-the-excel-depression.html

Kushner, M. G., Kim, S. W., Donahue, C., Thuras, P., Adson, D., Kotlyar, M., . . . Foa, E. B. (2007). D-cycloserine augmented exposure therapy for obsessive–compulsive disorder. *Biological Psychiatry*, *62*, 835–838. http://dx.doi.org/10.1016/j.biopsych.2006.12.020

LaCour, M. J., & Green, D. P. (2014, December 12). When contact changes minds: An experiment on transmission of support for gay equality. *Science*, *346*, 1366–1369. http://dx.doi.org/10.1126/science.1256151

Landesman, P. (Producer), Scott, R., Facio, G., Wolthoff, D., Shuman, L., & Cantillon, E. (Directors). (2015). *Concussion* [Motion picture]. United States: Columbia Pictures.

LibreOffice [Computer software]. Berlin, Germany: Document Foundation. Available from https://www.libreoffice.org/

Martindale, C. (1978). The therapist-as-fixed-effect fallacy in psychotherapy research. *Journal of Consulting and Clinical Psychology*, *46*, 1526–1530. http://dx.doi.org/10.1037/0022-006X.46.6.1526

Maxwell, S. E., & Delaney, H. D. (2004). *Designing experiments and analyzing data: A model comparison approach* (2nd ed.). Mahwah, NJ: Erlbaum.

McCloskey, D. N. (2000). *Economical writing*. Long Grove, IL: Waveland Press.

McCrone, P., Sharpe, M., Chalder, T., Knapp, M., Johnson, A. L., Goldsmith, K. A., & White, P. D. (2012). Adaptive pacing, cognitive behaviour therapy, graded exercise, and specialist medical care for chronic fatigue syndrome: A cost-effectiveness analysis. *PLOS ONE*, *7*, e40808. http://dx.doi.org/10.1371/journal.pone.0040808

McNally, R. J., Lasko, N. B., Clancy, S. A., Macklin, M. L., Pitman, R. K., & Orr, S. P. (2004). Psychophysiological responding during script-driven imagery in people reporting abduction by space aliens. *Psychological Science*, *15*, 493–497. http://dx.doi.org/10.1111/j.0956-7976.2004.00707.x

Mendeley [Computer software]. New York, NY: Author. Retrieved from https://www.mendeley.com

Mineka, S., & Zinbarg, R. (2006). A contemporary learning theory perspective on the etiology of anxiety disorders: It's not what you thought it was. *American Psychologist*, *61*, 10–26. http://dx.doi.org/10.1037/0003-066X.61.1.10

The 90% question. (2013). *The Economist*. Retrieved from http://www.economist.com/news/finance-and-economics/21576362-seminal-analysis-relationship-between-debt-and-growth-comes-under

Novella, S. (2014, April 30). Microwaves and nutrition. *Science-Based Medicine*. Retrieved from https://www.sciencebasedmedicine.org/microwaves-and-nutrition/

Orwell, G. (1946). Politics and the English language. Retrieved from http://www.orwell.ru/library/essays/politics/english/e_polit/

Page, J., & Plant, R. (1971). Stairway to heaven [Recorded by Led Zeppelin]. On *Led Zeppelin IV* [Vinyl]. New York, NY: Atlantic.

Pediatric OCD Treatment Study Team. (2004). Cognitive–behavior therapy, sertraline, and their combination for children and adolescents with obsessive–compulsive disorder: The Pediatric OCD Treatment Study (POTS) randomized controlled trial. *JAMA, 292,* 1969–1976. http://dx.doi.org/10.1001/jama.292.16.1969

Rachman, S., & Shafran, R. (1998). Cognitive and behavioral features of obsessive–compulsive disorder. In R. Swinson, M. Antony, S. Rachman, & M. Richter (Eds.), *Obsessive–compulsive disorder: Theory, research, and treatments* (pp. 51–78). New York, NY: Guilford Press.

Reiner, R. (Producer), Reiner, R., Brown, D., & Scheinman, A. (Directors). (1992). *A few good men* [Motion picture]. United States: Columbia Pictures.

Reinhart, C. M., & Rogoff, K. S. (2010). *Growth in a time of debt* (Working Paper No. 15639). Cambridge, MA: National Bureau of Economic Research. Retrieved from http://www.nber.org/papers/w15639

Rocksmith [Video game]. (2012). San Francisco, CA: Ubisoft.

Rocksmith: Audrey's success story [Video]. (2016). Retrieved from https://www.youtube.com/watch?v=qpeDWRu1ZvQ

Schwartz, J. M., & Beyette, B. (1997). *Brain lock: Free yourself from obsessive–compulsive disorder.* New York, NY: Regan Books.

Silvia, P. J. (2007). *How to write a lot: A practical guide to productive academic writing.* Washington, DC: American Psychological Association.

Simmons, J. P., Nelson, L. D., & Simonsohn, U. (2011). False-positive psychology: Undisclosed flexibility in data collection and analysis allows presenting anything as significant. *Psychological Science, 22,* 1359–1366. http://dx.doi.org/10.1177/0956797611417632

Simons, A. D., Garfield, S. L., & Murphy, G. E. (1984). The process of change in cognitive therapy and pharmacotherapy for depression. *Archives of General Psychiatry, 41,* 45–51.

Steel, P. (2007). The nature of procrastination: A meta-analytic and theoretical review of quintessential self-regulatory failure. *Psychological Bulletin, 133,* 65–94. http://dx.doi.org/10.1037/0033-2909.133.1.65

Steketee, G., & Barlow, D. H. (2002). Obsessive–compulsive disorder. In D. H. Barlow (Ed.), *Anxiety and its disorders* (2nd ed., pp. 516–560). New York, NY: Guilford Press.

Tanaka, T., Kikushima, R. (Producers), & Kurosawa, A. (Director). (1962). *Sanjuro* [Motion picture]. Japan: Toho.

Tanaka, T., Kikushima, R., Kurosawa, A. (Producers), & Kurosawa, A. (Director). (1961). *Yojimbo* [Motion picture]. Japan: Toho.

Thicke, R., Williams, P., Harris, C., Jr., & Gaye, M. (2013). Blurred lines [Recorded by R. Thicke, T. I., & P. Williams]. On *Blurred lines* [CD]. Virginia Beach, VA, & Santa Monica, CA: Star Trak & Interscope.

Tuesday, J. (2009). Famous movie quotes ruined by the passive voice [Web log post]. Retrieved from http://thislandisthailand.blogspot.com/2009/08/famous-movie-quotes-ruined-by-passive.html

Wampold, B. E., & Imel, Z. E. (2015). *The great psychotherapy debate: The evidence for what makes psychotherapy work* (2nd ed.). New York, NY: Routledge.

Wampold, B. E., & Serlin, R. C. (2000). The consequence of ignoring a nested factor on measures of effect size in analysis of variance. *Psychological Methods, 5,* 425–433. http://dx.doi.org/10.1037/1082-989X.5.4.425

Webb, C. A., DeRubeis, R. J., & Barber, J. P. (2010). Therapist adherence/competence and treatment outcome: A meta-analytic review. *Journal of Consulting and Clinical Psychology, 78,* 200–211. http://dx.doi.org/10.1037/a0018912

Weintraub, J. (Producer), & Avildsen, J. G. (Director). (1984). *The karate kid* [Motion picture]. United States: Columbia Pictures.

Wilson, R., Taylor, R., Wilson, R., Simmons, L., & Wilson, C. (1979). Oops upside your head [Recorded by The Gap Band]. On *The Gap Band II* [Vinyl]. Beverly Hills, CA, & New York, NY: Total Experience & Mercury.

Zinsser, W. (2006). *On writing well* (6th ed.). New York, NY: Harper Perennial.

Zotero [Computer software]. Fairfax, VA: Roy Rosenzweig Center for History and New Media. Retrieved from http://zotero.org

Index

About the Author

Scott A. Baldwin, PhD, received his doctorate in clinical psychology from the University of Memphis in 2006. He completed his predoctoral clinical internship at the University of Wisconsin–Madison Department of Psychiatry. He's an associate professor of psychology at Brigham Young University and a licensed psychologist in Utah.

Dr. Baldwin's research focuses on research design, statistical, and measurement issues in psychotherapy and health research. He has published more than 50 articles and has focused his recent efforts on demonstrating the use of advanced statistical methods in psychological research. He teaches courses on statistics, measurement, research design, and psychotherapy. When not doing data analysis or writing, he likes to spend time with his family, swim, bike, run, and play classic video games.

About the Series Editor

Arthur M. Nezu, PhD, DHL, ABPP, is Distinguished University Professor of Psychology, professor of medicine, and professor of public health at Drexel University. In addition to currently serving as an associate editor of *American Psychologist*, he has held several previous editorial positions, including editor of the *Journal of Consulting and Clinical Psychology*, associate editor of *Archives of Scientific Psychology*, editor of *The Behavior Therapist*, and chair of the Council of Editors for the American Psychological Association. His research and program development in clinical psychology and behavioral medicine have been supported by the National Cancer Institute, the National Institute of Mental Health, the Department of Veterans Affairs, the Department of Defense, the U.S. Air Force, and the Pew Fund. Dr. Nezu has also served on numerous research review panels for the National Institutes of Health and was previous president of both the Association of Behavioral and Cognitive Therapies and the American Board of Behavioral and Cognitive Psychology.